The Encyclopedia of
Motorcycles
Suzuki–ZZR

The Encyclopedia of Motorcycles
Sukuki–ZZR

Peter Henshaw

Chelsea House Publishers
Philadelphia

Published in 2000 by
Chelsea House Publishers
1974 Sproul Road, Suite 400
P.O. Box 914
Broomall. PA 19008-0914

ISBN 0-7910-6057-8

Printed in Singapore

Library of Congress Cataloging-in- Publication Data applied for

ABOVE, RIGHT and OPPOSITE: Suzuki concentrated on small two-strokes throughout the 1960s

SUZUKI *Japan 1952–*

If World War II had never occurred, Suzuki might well have beaten all its major home-grown rivals to first place in the motorcycle industry. In 1937, Soichiro Honda was concentrating on piston rings, Yamaha on making musical instruments and Kawasaki was still 23 years away from its first motorcycle. Yet in that year, Suzuki had built a prototype motorcycle engine, so it is clear that the company was contemplating the two-wheel market long before its contemporaries. That all four ended up building bikes were for the same pragmatic reasons: that they had seen their traditional markets disrupted or decimated because of war, and that post-war Japan was seeing an unprecedented demand for cheap two-wheeled transport.

Like its contemporaries, Suzuki did not start out as a motorcycle manufacturer at all. Michio Suzuki was born in February 1887, in the village of Hamamatsu, where the company is based to this day, though

now it is a general part of Japan's coastal industrial sprawl. Like Soichiro Honda, Michio was as much an entrepreneur as an engineer, and in 1909 at the age of 22 went into business on his own account, building silk looms.

The silk industry was important to Japan, being so widespread, so the new Suzuki company grew fast, even though its founder was seeking other diversifications, hence that prototype engine in 1937, and an agreement the same year to build the Austin Seven car under licence. But the war, and Japan's rearmament programme which preceded it, put a stop to any thoughts in that direction. Obliged to commit itself to the military machine, Suzuki was granted permission to recommence loom production by the American occupying forces in September 1945. Unfortunately, raw silk was by now very difficult to come by, and Suzuki's only means of survival was to look to other markets, which it did in the form of heaters, farm machinery and various other

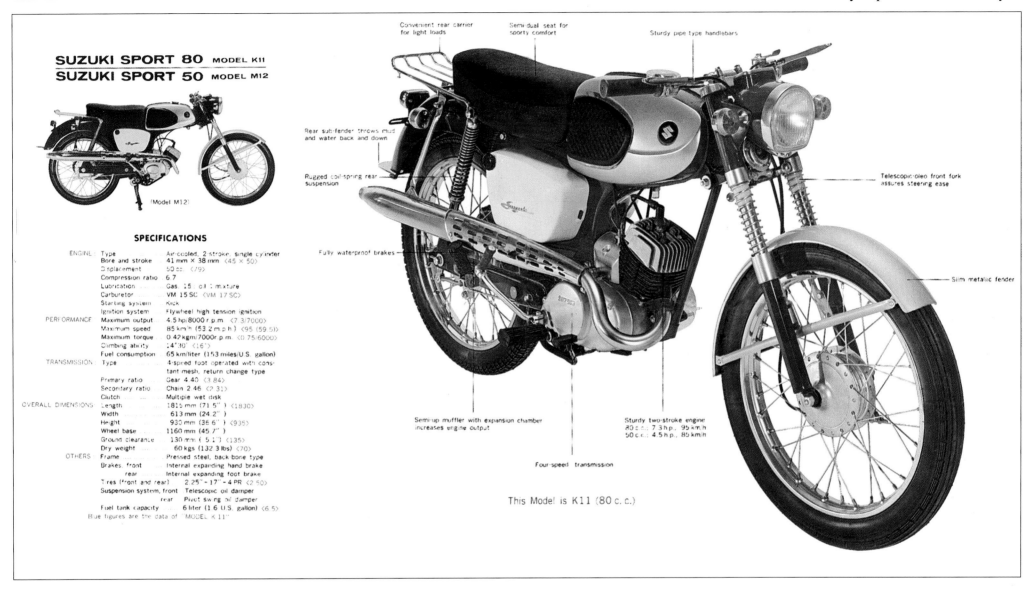

SUZUKI SPORT 80 MODEL K11
SUZUKI SPORT 50 MODEL M12

(Model M12)

Convenient rear carrier for light loads

Semi-dual seat for sporty comfort

Sturdy pipe type handlebars

Rear sub-fender throws mud and water back and down

Rugged coil-spring rear suspension

Telescopic-oleo front fork assures steering ease

Fully waterproof brakes

Slim metallic fender

Semi-up muffler with expansion chamber increases engine output

Sturdy two-stroke engine
80 c.c.: 7.3 h.p., 95 km/h
50 c.c.: 4.5 h.p., 85 km/h

Four-speed transmission

This Model is K11 (80 c.c.)

SPECIFICATIONS

ENGINE :	Type	Air-cooled, 2-stroke, single cylinder
	Bore and stroke	41 mm × 38 mm ⟨45 × 50⟩
	Displacement	50 c.c. ⟨79⟩
	Compression ratio	6.7
	Lubrication	Gas 15 : oil 1 mixture
	Carburetor	VM 15 SC ⟨VM 17 SC⟩
	Starting system	Kick
	Ignition system	Flywheel high tension ignition
PERFORMANCE	Maximum output	4.5 h.p/8000 r.p.m. ⟨7.3/7000⟩
	Maximum speed	85 km/h (53.2 m.p.h.) ⟨95 (59.5)⟩
	Maximum torque	0.42 kgm/7000 r.p.m. ⟨0.75/6000⟩
	Climbing ability	14°30′ ⟨16°⟩
	Fuel consumption	65 km/liter (153 miles/U.S. gallon)
TRANSMISSION :	Type	4-speed foot operated with constant mesh, return change type
	Primary ratio	Gear 4.40 ⟨3.84⟩
	Secondary ratio	Chain 2.46 ⟨2.31⟩
	Clutch	Multiple wet disk
OVERALL DIMENSIONS	Length	1815 mm (71.5″) ⟨1830⟩
	Width	613 mm (24.2″)
	Height	930 mm (36.6″) ⟨935⟩
	Wheel base	1160 mm (45.7″)
	Ground clearance	130 mm (5.1″) ⟨135⟩
	Dry weight	60 kgs (132.3 lbs) ⟨70⟩
OTHERS	Frame	Pressed steel, back-bone type
	Brakes : front	Internal expanding hand brake
	rear	Internal expanding foot brake
	Tires (front and rear)	2.25″ – 17″ – 4 PR ⟨2.50⟩
	Suspension system, front	Telescopic oil damper
	rear	Pivot swing oil damper
	Fuel tank capacity	6 liter (1.6 U.S. gallon) ⟨6.5⟩

Blue figures are the data of "MODEL K 11"

---

products which kept the company afloat for the next few years.

Michio Suzuki was well into his 60s when he decided upon the final solution that would set the seal on his company's fortunes. He was a keen fisherman and was accustomed to cycling to his favourite

fishing haunts; but he could also see the attraction of a motorized bicycle, designed to take the effort out of such trips. More importantly, he was also able to recognize the crucial connection with this and the country's rapidly growing demand for such transport. Perhaps, like the men behind

Lambretta, the Vespa and Harley-Davidson, he was simply there at the right time.

Work began on the first prototype in November 1951, a 36cc (2cu in) two-stroke clip-on unit which could be fitted to any bicycle. It went on sale seven months later, under the name of Power Free.

Significantly, it was all made in-house by Suzuki itself, which underlined the company's serious intent; this was no short-term attempt at making money on the back of the clip-on boom. Suzuki clearly intended to stay with the two-wheel market, and grow with it. The original Power Free was soon followed by the 60cc (4cu in) Diamond Free in March 1953. But the Diamond Free wasn't just a clip-on, and as a complete bike won its class in the 1953 Mount Fuji hillclimb.

This success (both in the marketplace and in racing) encouraged the company to produce its first complete road bike, and the Colleda ('This is it') was announced in May 1954. Now some say this was Suzuki's first four-stroke, others that it was a two-stroke. Whoever is right, it is certain that the 90cc (5.5cu in) single won the Mount Fuji hillclimb in its debut year. A bigger 125cc (8cu in) two-stroke, the Colleda ST, followed in 1955. By now, the clip-on engines had been dropped and Suzuki was becoming a mass-producer of small motorcycles. Two years later, a new plant and increased capacity made it second only to Honda in the Japanese market.

Just as significant at the time was Michio's son Shunzo's trip to North America, which convinced him that here was another huge market ripe for exploitation. Also, the Colleda's early competition success led to Suzuki's long (and still successful) association with racing. A special 125cc racer was built in 1955, though met with little success and it was another four years before a purpose-built racer (another 125, with 10bhp, a four-speed gearbox, telescopic forks and swinging-arm frame) ventured onto the tracks. The Colleda RB could only manage fifth in the 1959 Asama races (Honda was unassailable that year), but afterwards Soichiro Honda was to casually ask Shunzo Suzuki why they didn't race such a fast machine abroad. The following year, Suzuki was in the Isle of Man.

SUZUKI RV 125

Maximum Horsepower	9.8 hp/6,000 rpm S.A.E. NET
Maximum Torque	1.20 kg·m (8.68 ft-lb)/5,500 rpm
Engine Type	2-stroke, single cylinder
Piston Displacement	123 cc (7.5 cu·in)
Transmission	5-speed, constant mesh
Fuel Tank Capacity	4.7 ltr (1.2/1.0 US/Imp gal)
Lubrication	Suzuki CCI
Overall Length	1,960 mm (77.2 in)
Overall Width	835 mm (32.9 in)
Overall Height	1,055 mm (41.5 in)

Ground Clearance	165 mm (6.5 in)
Suspension, Front	Telescopic, oil dampened
Rear	Oil dampened, 3 way adjustable
Tires, Front	5.4-14-4PR
Rear	6.7-12-4PR
Dry Weight	111 kg (244 lbs)
Starter	Primary kick
Color	Marble scarlet
	Maui blue metallic

SUZUKI CCI
SUZUKI MOTOR CO., LTD.
300 Takatsuka, Hamamatsu, Japan

* Specifications subject to change without notice.

Printed in Japan

The RV125 was Suzuki"s answer to the Honda Monkey Bike

Pumps & Bloops

Although racing was important to Suzuki, just like its rivals it relied on small, simple commuter bikes as its mainstay. Typical were the K- and M-series machines of the early sixties, two-stroke singles which were made in huge numbers (Suzuki built over half a million of the K10 and K11 alone). Not that they were unsophisticated – all these bikes shared the attraction of oil injection. Instead of the usual petroil system, where the rider had to manually add the correct amount of two-stroke oil when filling up, the little Suzukis had separate oil tanks which automatically pumped lubricant directly to where it was needed, according to engine revs and throttle opening; the harder the engine worked, the more oil it got. With petroil, lubrication was a more haphazard affair where the petrol/oil mixture was sucked in

ABOVE: Suzuki DR400 trail bike

ABOVE RIGHT: The 100cc (6cu in) commuter with trail overtones

together and it was fingers crossed that sufficient oil reached the right parts! It may seem like an esoteric technical point, but Suzuki's CCI system (Controlled Crankshaft Injection) was really a huge step forward for non-enthusiasts, who could now fill up with pure petrol just as with any car.

The K- and M-series were replaced by the B100P of 1964. Nicknamed the 'Bloop', this 119cc (7.3cu in) two-stroke (with CCI of course) proved a long-running hit, and remained on sale until 1970. It was even revived in the mid-1970s as the B120 Student. Similarly long-lived was the smaller A100 of 1967, which survived right into the 1980s, while slightly bigger was the 246cc (15cu in) T10, which was a development of the 1956 Colleda TT (Suzuki's first twin-cylinder bike) and the Twinace models of 1960. Although mechanically similar, the 1963 T10 was

evidence of a new attack on export markets, with the electric start and indicators with which Japanese lightweights were making their mark. Surprisingly, considering Suzuki's imminent association with fearsome performance two-stroke twins, the T10 was mild-mannered, with a flat, gentle power curve and four-speed gearbox. With its pressed steel frame and Germanic styling, the T10 had all the appearance of the early Japanese bike that it was. However, something very different was to come.

Meanwhile, Suzuki had been making its mark in the West, not with mass-market sales, but in racing. Entries to the 1960 and '61 Isle of Man TTs had brought a best of 15 place. But it was Ernst Degner's controversial defection from MZ and East Germany to Suzuki in late 1961 that provided the real breakthrough; he brought

much of MZ's rotary-valve two-stroke know-how with him, and within months Suzuki had a competitive GP racer. Degner won the 50cc Championship the following year, and Hugh Anderson took the 125 class in 1963. Four more 50cc titles and two 125s were to follow up to 1970. A square four-cylinder 250 (based on two 125 twins in tandem) was less successful, though Suzuki was to return to the basic concept of a square-four two-stroke later on, with happier results.

While all this was going on, Suzuki's road bike range was basically non-sporting, but 1966 saw the launch of its first true sportsbike, which was also designed with an eye on export markets. The T20 Super Six (named the X6 in America) was much more than a tuned-up T10. In fact, it was completely different. Although it too was a 247cc two-stroke twin, the engine was

completely new, with alloy barrels, 24mm carburettors and a six-speed gearbox. To save weight, the electric start was omitted and the pressed steel frame was dispensed with in favour of 'proper' tubular steel. With 29bhp at its disposal, the Super Six could easily top 145km/h (90mph), and contemporary road tests waxed lyrical about a bike that set new standards in the 250 class. More than any other bike, the Super Six brought Suzuki to the attention of the European and American markets. It was evidently a success, for the company followed it up with the smaller T200 and larger T500 only a year later. The 500, in particular, won many friends, although it

didn't handle as well as the lighter 250, but 46bhp at 7,000rpm gave it a 177km/h (110mph) performance, so it was almost as fast but less frenetic than Kawasaki's manic two-stroke triple. The T500 (known as Titan in the United States, Cobra in Britain) enjoyed a long life, and survived until 1977 as the GT500 with front disc brake and electronic ignition.

There were also updates in the 250 twin theme (plus enlarged 305cc and 316cc/19cu inch inversions up to 1973) in the early/mid 1970s, culminating in the GT250X7, which claimed to be the first-ever 100mph production 250. (Ducati had actually

claimed the same for its Mach 3 a few years earlier, but no doubt the arguments will rage for years to come.) To supplement the popular 500 twin, Suzuki produced two-stroke triples of its own, the GT380 and GT550 from 1972; both were smoother and faster than the older bike and the six-speed 380 was something of a classic of its time, one of the last air-cooled performance two-strokes. They came complete with 'Ram Air', which sounded mighty impressive but was merely squared-off cylinder cowling. The thirstier 550 was dropped in 1977, its smaller brother a couple of years later. At the same time, and in the same style, there were GT125 and GT185 twins.

The early 1970s also saw Suzuki's first real trail bike. Like its rivals, it had already sold street scramblers (road bikes with high-level exhausts) but the all-new TS125 of 1971 was a true dual-purpose machine, and designed as such. It could reach 113km/h (70mph) on tarmac, but was easy to ride off it, and was so successful that it led to a whole family of TS trail bikes. Smaller TS50 and TS100 variants came first, both of them (unlike the 125) with rotary-valve induction. A TS250 followed which, with 23bhp at 6,500rpm, gave useful on-road performance, while the later TS185 and TS400s completed the family. The biggest TS was later dropped, but the smaller ones were gradually updated in the eighties and nineties, notably with water-cooling. Suzuki carried on making the bikes that were to be its mainstay, notably, of course, the two-stroke GP100/125 from 1978, which replaced the venerable B120 and was capable of 70mph, as well as a succession of step-thrus. The latter were clearly inspired by the success of Honda's Cub, and

ABOVE and BELOW: Different generations of two-stroke twins, the 1960s T10 and the late '70s GTX7

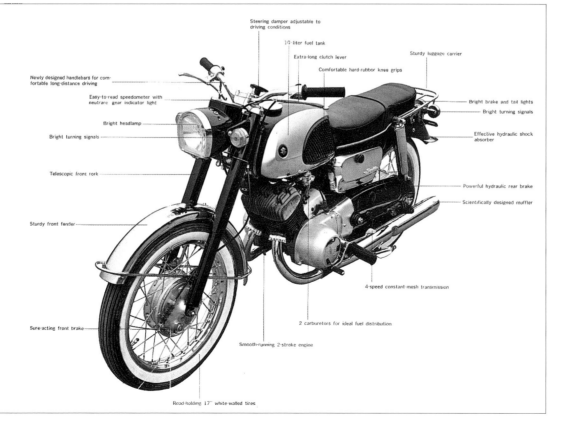

SUZUKI 250 MODEL T10

PERFORMANCE

The Suzuki 250 T10 performs like few cycles in its class. With its 2-cylinder, 2-carburetor, 21 h.p. engine, it wonderfully accelerates the first 400 meters only for 16.4 sec. Top speed is 140 km/h. Weighing only 140 kilograms, it is unrivaled in gas mileage — 45 kilometers on one liter of fuel.

Telescopic front fork and hydraulic rear shock absorbers make the Suzuki 250 T10 comfortable and easy-to-handle on rough roads, and its extra-long clutch and brake levers take the strain out of frequent stops and starts in heavy traffic. A special safety feature is the hydraulic rear brakes, shared by no other cycle in this class. Night driving is made safer with bright head and tail lights and turning signals.

These are only a few of the many outstanding performance characteristics of this marvelous machine, so get the whole story from your local dealer.

SPECIFICATIONS

ENGINE : Type ....Air-cooled, 2-stroke, twin cylinder
Bore and stroke ......52 mm × 58 mm
Displacement ....246 cc.
Compression ratio 6.3
Lubrication ....Gas. 15: oil 1 mixture
Carburetor ....VM 20, two
Starting system ....Starter dynamo with kick
Ignition system ......Battery ignition

PERFORMANCE : Maximum output ....21 hp/7000 r.p.m.
Maximum speed ....140 km/h (87 m.p.h.)
Maximum torque ....2.1 kg-m/7000 r.p.m.
Climbing ability ......18°
Fuel consumption ...45 kms/liter (105 miles/U.S. gallon)

TRANSMISSION : Type ....4-speed foot operated with constant-mesh, return change type
Primary ratio ....Gear 3.29
Secondary ratio .....Chain 2.50
Clutch ....Multiple wet disk

OVERALL DIMENSIONS : Length ....2065 mm (81.3″)
Width ....800 mm (31.5″)
Height ....1050 mm (41.3″)
Wheel base ....1350 mm (53.2″)
Ground clearance ...135 mm (5.31″)
Dry weight ....140 kgs (308.7 lbs)

OTHERS : Frame ....Pressed steel, back-bone type
Brakes front ....Internal expanding hand brake
rear ....Internal expanding foot brake
Tires (front and rear) ......3.00″—17″—4 PR
Suspension system front...Telescopic oil damper
rear ...Pivot swing oil damper
Fuel tank capacity ....10 liters (2.64 U.S. gallons)

Steering damper adjustable to driving conditions

10-liter fuel tank

Extra-long clutch lever

Sturdy luggage carrier

Comfortable hard-rubber knee grips

Newly designed handlebars for comfortable long-distance driving

Easy-to-read speedometer with neutrare gear indicator light

Bright brake and tail lights

Bright turning signals

Bright headlamp

Bright turning signals

Effective hydraulic shock absorber

Telescopic front fork

Powerful hydraulic rear brake

Sturdy front fender

Scientifically designed muffler

4-speed constant-mesh transmission

Sure-acting front brake

2 carburetors for ideal fuel distribution

Smooth-running 2-stroke engine

Road-holding 17″ white-walled tires

A 1978 GN250, the archetypal factory custom

looked very similar, the important difference being a two-stroke engine rather than the unfamiliar (to Suzuki) four-stroke, and 50cc and 70cc variants were offered.

Rotary, Big Four-Strokes

The story of Suzuki in the early/mid-1970s was of a search for alternatives to the air-cooled two-stroke, for big bikes at least. The success of Honda's CB750 and Kawasaki's Z1, not to mention the first fuel crisis and tighter emissions regulations, were making big, thirsty two-strokes untenable. This presented Suzuki with a problem, wedded as it was to the two-stroke

principle, and it wasn't until 1976 that it bowed to the inevitable and produced a big four-stroke of its own. In the meantime, there was the GT750 of 1969, Suzuki's immediate response to the 750cc (46cu in) Hondas and Kawasakis. Although a two-stroke triple, Suzuki's entrant was very different to the hair-raising Kawasaki H1. It was water-cooled, quiet and well-mannered, not over-tuned, but it still equalled the four-stroke Honda with 67bhp. Despite the 'GT' tag, the 750 (or 'Kettle' as it was known in Britain) was more of a smooth, comfortable tourer, being too heavy to rival sportier machines for

handling. It lasted seven years. Shorter-lived, but more radical, was Suzuki's rotary-engined RE5, which was unveiled at the Cologne Motorcycle Show in 1974. Unlike the simpler air-cooled rotaries being developed by DKW and Norton, the water-cooled RE5 looked monstrously complicated. It was heavy (245kg/540lb), produced less power than the GT750 and drank more fuel. It was not a success.

Fortunately for Suzuki (which lost a great deal of money with the RE5) better was to come. The GS750, launched in 1976, couldn't have been more different from the brave but flawed RE5. Instead, it was a thorough reworking of the big air-cooled four-cylinder concept popularized by Honda and Kawasaki. It was inevitable that the Suzuki GS750 would be a little faster than the Honda at 201km/h/125mph (thanks to twin overhead camshafts and a shorter stroke, power was 68bhp at 8,500rpm, with 44lb ft of torque at 7,000rpm). What set it apart was respectable handling. Until then, it was almost a truism that you couldn't have a high-horsepower Japanese four and good handling as well, but the GS750 broke this 'rule' with a relatively stiff frame that placed it well ahead of Honda. The result was a success for Suzuki, who followed it up with the 997cc (61cu in) GS1000 the year after. Suzuki's biggest bike yet produced 87bhp and could manage 217km/h (135mph), but it too handled well by the standards of the day and had adjustable suspension. It was no wonder that Suzuki's copywriters came up with the line, 'The lightweight heavyweight'. All sorts of variations on the GS1000 theme followed, notably the shaft-driven G version, and it lasted until 1981 when both it and the 750

were replaced by the four-valve GSX series.

Both GS750 and 1000 were the big sportsters of their day, but the GS850 was different. It was Suzuki's first purpose-designed tourer, and an attempt to grasp a slice of the touring market so successfully exploited by Honda with the Gold Wing. The 850 (it was announced in 1979) owed much to the 750, but was bored out to 843cc (51.4cu in) to produce 79bhp at 8,500rpm. The extra power was there to cope with the 850's extra weight (40kg/88lb more than the 750), much of which was down to the adoption of shaft-drive. Gas and rubber dampers were added to the transmission to minimize the clunky gearchange then associated with shaft-drive. The 850 was replaced by the GS1000G in 1980 which in turn became the 1100G in 1983. Suzuki was evidently getting the hang of four-stroke design, replacing all its mid-range two-strokes with fours in the mid/late 1970s. Alongside the GS750 it had unveiled a GS400 twin, with gear-driven balance-shaft. It looked little different from the rival CB/Z/XS400 twins but evolved into a long-lived line of reliable, ride-to-work bikes. The 400 soon became a 425 (in 1979) then a 450 (1980) and returned as the GS500 in 1989. Now with a more modern chassis, but the same basic two-valve air-cooled twin-cylinder motor, it offered cheap, basic motorcycling with reasonable performance. The four-cylinder GS550 from 1977 acquired a similar reputation for toughness, due to the use of roller bearings in the engine and a gear primary-drive. Like many Suzukis, its cosmetic qualities didn't always match up to its mechanics, but that didn't deter the buyers. Suzuki's four-stroke conversion affected its trail bikes as well.

ABOVE: GT125   BELOW: GT500   BELOW RIGHT: GT550   ABOVE: *The GSX400 was Suzuki's second-generation four-stroke twin*

The SP370 of 1978 led the change, perhaps in part inspired by Yamaha's XT500, and had 25bhp at 7,500rpm. It was soon enlarged into the SP400, but far bigger trail bikes were to come, starting with the DR600 in 1984. This was far in advance of the SP, with a twin-plug four-valve head, and 44bhp. If that wasn't enough, a DR750 was unveiled three years later, which eventually became the 780cc (48cu in) DR800, and the biggest single on sale, though it failed to deliver its early promise.

What made far more sense was the DR350 of 1991. Now here was a genuine dual-purpose bike, big enough to give useful on-road performance, but light and sufficiently wieldy to be rideable on dirt. Like Yamaha's XT350, the mid-range DR (there was also a 125 and 650) proved for many riders to be the best compromise

GS550 (this one with Dunstall extras) extended the four-cylinder range

GT380 gave smooth two-stroke performance

between power, weight, road and off-road use, which is what trail bikes are all about. By then, Suzuki had already proved it was well able to design sohc four-stroke singles for the road, with the custom-styled GN250/400 and the neat GS125 commuter.

16-Valve Debut

If the GS-series represented Suzuki's four-stroke revolution, then the GSX was the second generation that took it through the 1980s. It began in 1980 with the launch of the GSX1100 and 750. Their main innovation was the four-valve TSCC ('Twin Swirl Combustion Chamber') head, with a square-profiled combustion chamber designed to maximize swirl and thus combustion. The result was 100bhp for the 1100, which seemed impressive at the time. This was backed up by adjustable

air damping for the telescopic forks, and lumpy, angular styling with a rectangular headlamp. Not everyone liked the way the new bikes looked, and Suzuki responded with the more radical-looking Katanas in 1981. With low bars and small pointed fairings, they certainly transformed the looks of the GSX, and were available with a number of different four-cylinder engines over the years, from 250 to 1100cc (15 to 67cu in).

The 550 four also got the GSX 16-valve treatment in 1983, with power up to 65bhp, enough for a claimed 201km/h (125mph). It also acquired a new alloy square section frame, a half-fairing, monoshock rear suspension and anti-dive front forks. At the same time, the 750 and 1100 were sold in updated ES form, with 83 and 111bhp respectively. Naturally,

four-valve heads made their way into the twins as well as the GSX250 and 400, along with (again) more angular styling, and 177km/h (110mph) was claimed for the 400. The mid-1980s was also the time when a few manufacturers flirted with the idea of turbocharging, to give big bike power in a smaller, lighter package. Suzuki's offering was the XN85 Turbo, based on the existing air-cooled four which, in practice, produced 85bhp at the cost of extra complication, which wasn't enough. But really, the Turbo disclosed the fact that Suzuki's air-cooled four was nearing the end of its development life. The final 123bhp GSX1100E was certainly fast, but times had moved on, and Suzuki had another new generation to satisfy; it was the oil/air-cooled GSXR.

The GSXR Milestone

The 'race replica' as we understand it today (a powerful four-cylinder motor hung from an alloy perimeter frame, with a lean-forward race-style riding position) originated in the mid-1980s, and it is arguable that Suzuki was there first with the GSXR series. Although some might say that Yamaha's FZ750 has much of the same elements, the Suzuki GSXR750 was much more of a true race replica, being very close to the company's works endurance racers of the early eighties. By this time, Suzuki had established an enviable racing record, notably with the square-four RG500, which did so well in Grand Prix racing in the late 1970s/early '80s. Riders like Barry Sheene, Keith Heuwen, Graeme Crosby and Franco Uncini (and later Kevin Schwantz on the V4 RGV500) brought many race wins. In 1983,

Water-cooling was tried on Suzuki's GT750 to compete with the big four-strokes. It was smooth but heavy

Like its rivals, Suzuki's custom bikes took the V-twin route

the company won the World Endurance Championship and the GSXR, unveiled in September 1984, was simply a means of capitalizing on the fact.

What marked it out from all previous Suzukis was the use of oil-cooling. The four-cylinder engine was still partly air-cooled, but oil played the bigger role. It used two oil pumps to double the flow rate, while the underside of each piston crown was cooled by an oil jet, and there was of course a large oil cooler. Thin, tightly-packed cylinder fins further helped heat dissipation, as did a magnesium cam cover. The result of all this was a compact, relatively light engine (Suzuki said water-

cooling would have added 5kg/11lb) that produced 100bhp at 10,500rpm. Coupled with a remarkably low all-up weight (175.5kg/387lb) – partly due to the new frame, which weighed half as much as the old steel one – this gave the new bike stunning performance.

Not that it was perfect. In fact, the early GSXR750 suffered from a peaky power delivery that offered little urge below 7,000rpm and everything thereafter – torque peaked at 10,000rpm! Nor was the handling all that it should have been, with some riders complaining of a high speed weave despite that state-of-the-art frame and suspension. Still, none of that mattered to

the buyers. Here was a bike that offered real excitement, seemed genuinely new and to all intents and purposes looked like a road-going version of the endurance racer. It sold well, and established a new class – the race replica.

A more acceptable form of GSXR was the 1100 of 1987, with the same oil-cooled concept, but with its 1052cc (64cu in) four in a less frenetic state of tune. In practice, with its much broader spread of power, the bigger bike was easier to ride in traffic. And of course it was fast, with its much broader spread of power and 249km/h (155mph) was a genuine top speed. But the 750 did succeed as a clubman's racer, which was part of the original intention. The addition of factory racing parts made it competitive in Superbike and Superstock racing. In fact, so popular was the GSXR concept that 250,

400 and 600cc (15, 24 and 37cu in) versions followed, the smaller bikes being mainly for the restricted Japanese market. However, the 600 did well in the burgeoning European Supersports 600 arena. As with the 750, the Suzuki GSXR soon earned a reputation as wild boy of the 600 bunch – the uncompromising race replica to Honda's more civilized CBR600. All the GSXRs were gradually improved over the years, and by 1998 the 750 had gained fuel injection, water cooling and 135bhp.

Just as Suzuki based the GSXR's appeal on endurance racers, so the RG250 owed something to the two-stroke GP bikes. The company had been campaigning the V-twin two-strokes in 250 and 500 GP racing for some time, so road-going equivalents made some sense. Naturally, the RG250 and 500 were very light and fearsomely fast, the 250

GSX1100, which used four valves per cylinder

ABOVE: GSX1100G offered shaft-drive, but no fairing

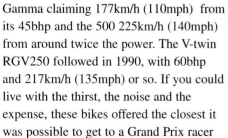

LEFT: The Bandit 600 was a huge success

ABOVE: Burgman 250 super-scooter

Gamma claiming 177km/h (110mph) from its 45bhp and the 500 225km/h (140mph) from around twice the power. The V-twin RGV250 followed in 1990, with 60bhp and 217km/h (135mph) or so. If you could live with the thirst, the noise and the expense, these bikes offered the closest it was possible to get to a Grand Prix racer

on the road.

But among all the race replicas, Suzuki took care to cater for the more sensible end of the market as well. The GSX600F and an equivalent 750 were fairly basic sports tourers, using a development of the air-cooled four and aiming at a budget-priced alternative to bikes like the Honda CBR600.

Announced in 1989, they had a substantial revamp in 1998. Also from 1993 there was an upgraded, more powerful RF600F, still in the sports tourer mode but with a higher specification (a similar 900cc/55cu inch version ran alongside it, and both are still on sale). A new top-of-the-range tourer was announced in 1988, the GSX1100F. Notable

for its electrically adjustable screen, the 1100 also represented the first use of Suzuki's oil-cooled four outside the GSXR sportsters. A slight capacity increase to 1127cc (69cu in) and much detuning saw 120bhp and a claimed 241km/h (150mph), but unfortunately the handling suffered from 16-inch wheels, and this GSX failed to have the impact of rivals such as Kawasaki's ZZR1100. There was also an unfaired GSX1100G, in the old 1000G tradition. Also, and of limited impact, was the VX800, using Suzuki's 800cc (49cu in) air-cooled V-twin from the cruiser range (750 and 1400cc/46 and 85cu inch versions of which were sold in the late 1980s) which added shaft-drive and conservative styling with a long wheelbase. Some traditionalists quite liked it.

An All-Round Winner

But if its tourers didn't always hit the mark, Suzuki did better in other areas. By the early 1990s, the 600cc class had become dominated by the super sportsters – bikes like the GSXR, in fact. But exciting as these machines were, they were hard work and uncomfortable to ride in traffic and difficult for those starting (or returning to) motorcycling late in life, of which there were increasing numbers. What was needed was a simpler, more accessible all-rounder, and Suzuki hit the nail on the head with the Bandit 600 in 1995. The Bandit used a detuned version of the GSXR600's oil-cooled engine, housed in a steel tubular frame. The rider sat upright on a naked, almost traditional-looking bike with no hint of race pretensions. It was easy to ride and with 80-odd bhp, was still fast enough for many riders. It went straight to the top of the sales charts. Part of the Bandit's success was that it actually looked very good, particularly in non-faired form, as the close-finned oil-cooled engine made an attractive lump. The Bandit was soon joined by a part-faired version, and the 1157cc (71cu in) Bandit 1200 was again in naked and part-faired guise. Such was the

The RF-series (both 600 and 900) was Suzuki's stab at the sports-touring market

Pat Hennan racing a 1978 Suzuki 500 at the Isle of Man TT

Bandit's success that it encouraged Honda (with the Hornet) and Yamaha (the Fazer) to produce their own equivalents.

But Suzuki's heart evidently lay in sportsbikes, as illustrated by the TL1000 V-twin sportster of late 1997. It was really an attempt to beat Ducati at its own game. The Italian marque had been riding the crest of a wave through the 1990s, thanks to racing success and new owners, and here was a chance for the Japanese to produce a cheaper, more user-friendly sports V-twin. The twin-cam, fuel-injected eight-valve V-twin produced 125bhp, weighed 187kg (412lb) and promised to be a Ducati with convenience. It was certainly exciting to ride, but perhaps too much so, and Honda's version – the VTR1000 Firestorm – was certainly less demanding. A slightly more powerful, but very different under the skin TL1000R followed in 1998, intended to form the basis of Suzuki's new V-twin Superbike contender. Introduced that year was also something very different, the 250cc (15.3cu in) Burgman superscooter. In the same mould as the Yamaha Majesty, it offered better handling and slightly more performance, while its bigger all-round build pointed towards the 400cc (24.4cu in) version, which was launched the following year. The Burgman 400 is currently the biggest scooter on sale, and with a claimed 100mph top speed offers true motorcycle performance.

The Burgman might claim to be the fastest scooter of all, but another new Suzuki did the same for motorcycles in 1999. It certainly had more power than anything else, and talk of it dominated the motorcycle press for months, the Hayabusa GSXR1300R hinting at a top speed of

ABOVE: GSX1300R Hayabusa – 200mph?   *BELOW: V650S V-twin*

Suzuki's TL1000S V-twin got off to a shaky start, but was soon supplemented by the 1000R

ABOVE: GSXR750 – the first of the real race replicas

BELOW: A 1991 Suzuki RGV250

322km/h (200mph). The figures alone said all that was necessary: 173bhp, 102lb ft, 0–60mph in 2.75 seconds, to 225km/h (140mph) in 10 seconds. Would it reach the 200mph mark? That seemed to be the question on everyone's lips in the spring of 1999, and at the time of writing no one has managed to find out either way. Still, the Hayabusa (a Japanese falcon that allegedly reaches that speed when diving) showed not only that the horsepower race was not yet over, but that Suzuki was also out there in front.

But just as everyone was getting over the Hayabusa, Suzuki launched a bike that was undeniably less spectacular, but probably more relevant to more riders. By the late 1990s, the Bandit 600 was increasingly coming under fire from younger competition, and Suzuki's answer was an all-new all-rounder, the SV650. It was a V-twin, slim and lightweight, that came in naked guise and with a more sporting half-fairing and lower bars. The first promised to be a lighter, handier Bandit, with added V-twin character; the second a mini-TL1000.

SUZY *France 1932–33*
A fully-enclosed 498cc (30cu in) ohc Chaise single, unit-constructed.

SWAN *England 1911–13*
Similar to the Neracar, it used a 499cc Precision single and had leaf-sprung rear suspension.

SYMPLEX *England 1913–22*
Used 311cc (19cu in) Dalm two-strokes.

SYPHAX *France 1952–53*
Produced 98–174cc (6-11cu in) two- and four-strokes with AMC or Aubier-Dunne engines.

T

TANDON *England 1948–57*
Used a large range of Villiers engines up to the 322cc (20cu in) twin.

TAPELLA-FUCHS *Italy 1953–57*
Fuchs-powered mopeds.

TAS *Germany 1924–31*
Produced 173cc (11cu in) two-strokes to 498cc (30cu in) four-strokes, with a variety of bought-in engines.

TAURA *Italy 1927–30*
Used JAP and Blackburne power units.

TAURUS *Italy 1933–66*
Made various singles of 173cc–496cc (11–30cu in) before the war, including a dohc racer, with more utilitarian two-strokes and ohv singles after 1945.

TAUTZ *Germany 1921–23*
A DKW-powered 118cc (7.2cu in) scooter.

TAVERNIER *France 1921–23*
Utilized a range of bought-in engines from Zurcher, JAP, and Blackburne.

TECO *Germany 1920–26*
Used Alba and Kühne engines to 346cc (21cu in).

TEDDY *France 1922–24*
203cc (12.4cu in) lightweights.

TEE-BEE *England 1908–11*
Used own and JAP's 293cc (18cu in) sv.

TEHUELCHE *Argentina 1958–62*
A 75cc (4.6cu in) ohv, many parts being imported from Italy.

TEMPLE *England 1924–28*
Part of the OEC range.

TEMPO *Norway 1949–*
Bought-in two-strokes of up to 123cc (7.5cu in). Now distributes mopeds.

TERRA *Germany 1922–24*
Own two-stroke of 127–172cc (8–10.5cu in).

TERROT *France 1901–61*
France's leading manufacturer for some time, it used various bought-in four-strokes in the early years, plus its own 175–250cc (11–15cu in) two-strokes after World War I. Then came its own four-strokes from 1927, including a 750cc (46cu in) V-twin from 1930. After 1945 it continued its pre-war 498cc (30cu in) single, but most production lay in two-stroke lightweights up to 175cc, including a scooter. It had increasingly strong links with Automoto (part of Peugeot) in the late 1950s until Peugeot took over altogether in 1961.

TERROT *Czechoslovakia 1933–35*
Subsidiary of the French Terrot, with a 346cc (21cu in) sv.

TESTI *Italy 1951–83*
Used bought-in 49cc (3cu in) two-strokes on mopeds and small sportsters. Also exported with Horex or Gitane badges and had limited production alongside OMC from 1987.

TETGE *Germany 1923–26*
Produced 148/172cc (9/10.5cu in) singles, and a MAG-powered V-twin.

THIEM *U.S.A. 1903–14*
Typically offered American 550cc (34cu in) ioe singles and 890 or 996cc (54 or 61cu in) V-twins.

THOMANN *France 1912–39*
Made two-strokes from 98–248cc (6–15cu in).

THOMAS *U.S.A. 1900–08*
A 3hp 'sloper' single.

THOMAS *England 1904*
Used Minerva and Sarolea units.

THOR *U.S.A. 1903–16*
Produced its own 6 and 9hp machines, but mainly sold its ioe V-twins to other manufacturers.

THOROUGH *England 1903*
Used MMC and Coronet engines.

THREE-SPIRES *England 1931–32*
A 147cc (9cu in) two-stroke for 18 guineas – cheap at the price, no doubt.

THUMANN *Germany 1925–26*
Built own 246/346cc (15/21cu in) sv singles.

THUNDER *Italy 1952–54*
An advanced but expensive 127cc (8cu in)

Thor made its own engines and sold most of them to other manufacturers

twin with unit-construction, swinging-arm rear suspension and four-speed gearbox.

TIGER *U.S.A. 1915–16*
Used a 241cc (15cu in) two-stroke.

TIKA *Germany 1921–24*
Used a bought-in 145/195cc (9/12cu in) Herko sv.

TILBROOK *Australia 1950–53*
Made Villiers-engined lightweights to 198cc (12cu in).

TILSTON *England 1919*
A short-lived 225cc (14cu in) Precision-engined two-stroke.

TITAN *Austria 1927–33*
Produced both two- and four-strokes, notably a 144cc (9cu in) twin.

TIZ-AM *Russia 1913–40*
596cc (36cu in) sv singles.

TM *Italy 1968–92*
Made lightweights to 123cc (7.5cu in), first with Franco-Morini and Zündapp engines, later with its own.

TOHATSU *Japan 1935–66*
48–248cc (3–15cu in) disc-valved two-strokes.

TOMASELLI *Italy 1931–39*
173–490cc (11–30cu in) JAP-engined singles.

TOMMASI *Italy 1926–27*
Used Della Ferrera two-strokes, the 246cc (15cu in) version being two singles coupled together.

TOMOS *Slovenia 1954–*
Began with licence-built Puchs and later developed its own mopeds, plus a few larger bikes of up to 175cc (11cu in).

TOREADOR *England 1924–26*
Used bought-in engines from Bradshaw, JAP and MAG.

TORNAX *Germany 1926–55*
Pre-war, utilized a range of bought-in four-strokes up to a 996cc (30cu in) JAP, plus the Columbus 598/698cc (36/43cu in) ohc vertical twin. After 1945, produced mostly Ilo-engined two-strokes.

TORPADO *Italy 1950–62*
38–74cc (2.3–4.5cu in) Mosquito and Minarelli-engined two-strokes.

TORPEDO *Germany 1901–07*
Used Zedel and Fafnir engines.

TORPEDO *Czechoslovakia 1903–12*
Nearly everything was built in-house for this range of singles and V-twins up to 8hp.

TORPEDO *England 1910–20*
Precision singles and V-twins up to 499cc (30cu in).

TORPEDO *Germany 1928–56*
Used bought-in Blackburne, Sachs and Ilo power units.

TORROT *Spain 1960–85*
Began as a Terrot subsidiary and went on to build its own mopeds and lightweights.

TOWNEND *England 1901–04*
2/2.5hp engines.

TOYOMOTOR *Japan 1949–59*
Initially produced a motorized bicycle which was actually Japan's third best-seller by 1952. Later, an Adler-inspired two-stroke twin failed to save it.

TRAFALGAR *England 1902–05*
Used MMC and Minerva engines.

TRAFFORD *England 1919–22*
Used 269cc (16cu in) Villiers engines.

TRAIN *France 1913–39*
Built a complete range of engines, from a 173cc (11cu in) two-stroke to a 996cc (30cu in) V-twin, and supplied countless small assemblers (mostly in France and Italy) with ready-made power units. Also built an ohc in-line four in 1930, and was an early user of unit-construction.

TREBLOC *England 1922–25*
Built its own 63cc/3.8cu inch-engined lightweight.

TREMO *Germany 1925–28*
Own 308cc (19cu in) single with sv or ohv.

TRENT *England 1902–c.1906*
A 207cc (13cu in) engine in a strengthened cycle frame.

TRESPEDI *Italy 1926–30*
Own 173/246cc (11/15cu in) three-port two-strokes.

TRIANON *Germany 1922–26*
Own 232cc (14cu in) two-stroke.

TRIBUNE *U.S.A. 1903–c.1914*
Little is known, but Aster and Thor engines were possibly used.

TRIPLE-H *England 1921–23*
246cc (15cu in) two-strokes.

TRIPLETTE *England 1923–25*
A 147cc (9cu in) Villiers-powered utility.

TRIPOL *Czechoslovakia 1925–26*
Utilized a 246cc (15cu in) Villiers engine.

TRIUMPH *England 1903–*
It is odd that Triumph, who produced that most British of bikes, should have actually been established by two Germans, Mauritz Schulte and Siegfried Bettmann who, emigrating to England from their home town of Nuremberg, ended up in Coventry. Bettmann teamed up with Schulte in 1897 to make bicycles, and it was only five years before the fledgling Triumph produced its first motorized cycle. Whether their original intention was to set up as motorcycle manufacturers, history does not record, but they couldn't have chosen a better location in which to do so. With its long history of light engineering and central position in Britain's industrial West Midlands, Coventry offered several generations of craftsmen with the right skills and know-how useful to the nascent motorcycle industry.

Schulte and Bettmann's first effort resembled a bicycle rather than a motorbike, but this was no different from countless others. There was good reason for this: it was no more nor less than an adapted bicycle frame with an engine bolted on, though strengthened with a vertical brace on the front forks. Like many rivals, the Triumph founders chose to buy in an engine, in this case a Belgian-made Minerva of 239cc (14.6cu in) and 2.25bhp.

Early manufacturers tried various positions for these little bolt-on power units, but Triumph's was close to the standard motorcycle position, fixed to the frame's downtube. A slim tank inside the frame held fuel, oil and a battery. Transmission was by direct belt-drive, so to start it was necessary to pedal up to speed until the engine fired. Once running, the Minerva-engined Triumph would top about 40km/h (25mph).

Other proprietory engines followed, notably from JAP and Fafnir, before Schulte produced Triumph's first in-house design. It was an unremarkable sidevalve single of 3.5hp which was however to power Triumphs for some time. It started out at 499cc (30cu in), though a longer-stroke 547cc (33cu in) version later became available. Success in the TT (Jack Marshall won the 1908 single-cylinder class) underlined Triumph's arrival as one of the major manufacturers, as did World War I, when despatch riders learned to love their 'Trusty Triumphs'.

Other models followed, notably the two-stroke 225cc (13.7cu in) Baby, and the company demonstrated that it wasn't averse to innovation when a 496cc vertical twin was produced in prototype form as early as 1913 (20 years before Val Page's first production twin) and the early twenties saw a 346cc (21cu in) single with unit-construction. Perhaps most famous was the 'Riccy', the four-valve 499cc single designed by Harry Ricardo, a classic sports machine of its time which lasted until 1926 and was succeeded by a simpler two-valve 500.

It is often forgotten that there were close links between the British and German Triumph factories in those days. Coventry supplied many components, including engines, to Nuremburg until 1929 when the two finally went their separate ways.

Triumph motorcycles very nearly died a death in the 1930s. The parent company was more interested in four wheels than two, and had already sold off the bicycle side of the business to Raleigh. It was a golden opportunity to pick up a well established company for a song, and here two men were to become crucial to Triumph's existence. Jack Sangster was an astute businessman who had bought the bike side of Ariel from the receiver a few years earlier. His forward design engineer was someone who would be central to the Triumph story for the next 30 years – Edward Turner.

Much has been written of Turner, not all of it complimentary. He was the classic flawed genius, at times brilliant and far-sighted, at other times difficult, irascible and impatient. Although he had designed several significant bikes, notably the Triumph Speed Twin and the Ariel Square Four, he was more of an ideas man than an engineer. He was lacking in formal engineering training and Bert Hopwood (his protégé and a qualified engineer) suspected him of often preferring gut feeling to science, liable to dismiss anyone using a slide rule as an 'academic'. It became the norm at Triumph, Hopwood was later to report, to have two sets of drawings for every part – Turner's, and a set which had been painstakingly corrected and were the ones which were used in actual production. Turner, of course, knew nothing of this, which was probably just as well. On the other hand, he had tremendous energy and enthusiasm and a well developed aesthetic sense, together with a genuine feel for what the riding public really wanted.

ABOVE and OPPOSITE: An early belt-drive Triumph, the kind used by despatch riders in World War I

'Trusty Triumphs' were (and are) simple and easy to ride

ABOVE and BELOW: In order to help sales, Edward Turner spruced up Triumph's singles

In short, he was the right man arriving at the right time to revive the ailing Triumph concern and at the age of 35 was placed in charge of the new Triumph Engineering Company. His first job was to revamp Triumph's well-engineered but lacklustre range. The singles were given the Turner treatment, with a little more power, a curvaceous silver-and-chrome tank, and high-level exhausts. There were new names, too: the 250, 350 and 500 singles were now the Tiger 70, 80 and 90 respectively, the numbers suggesting their top speeds which was decidedly optimistic. But that didn't matter, as they fitted in with Triumph's new sporting image, which Turner was particularly adept at encouraging. Not surprisingly, Val Page's solid but slow 6/1 was dropped and even the Triumph logo was given the Turner touch. Aided by a general recovery in the motorcycle market, Triumph sales grew apace.

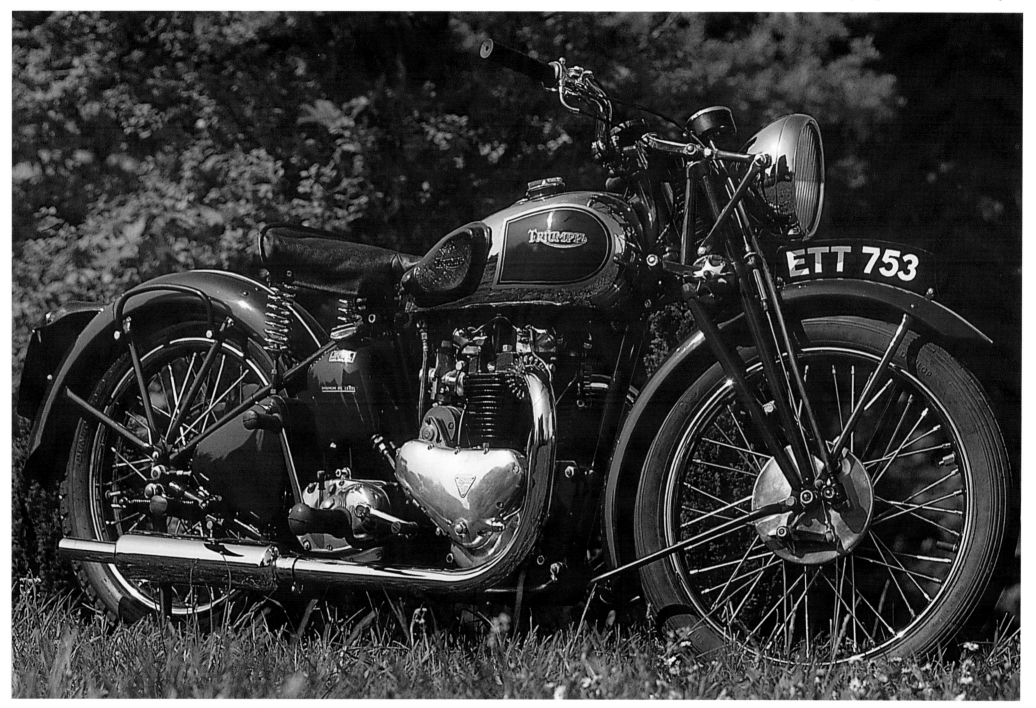

Triumph's milestone machine, the 1937 Speed Twin, transformed the company's fortunes and every major rival followed suit

The Twin

All this, however, was more of a holding operation before Turner's Big Idea for Triumph was ready, the Speed Twin, which was unveiled in July 1937. There had been twins before, but nothing like this; most were big, lumbering sidecar tugs with zero sporting potential. The Speed Twin weighed only 2.3kg (5lb) more than Triumph's existing Tiger 90 single; it was revvy and quick off the mark in a way that no other sporting single had been and, in its

The 1971 Bandit was meant to be a new-generation twin. It never made it

TR5 in ISDT trim

The late-model Sports Cub introduced many to motorcycling

LEFT: A 1965 Bonneville and one from 1971 (RIGHT)

original mild tune (a small carburettor and 7.2:1 compression), relatively smooth as well. Despite the mild tune, it produced 29bhp at 6,000rpm, enough for a top speed of 137–145km/h (85–90mph).

Even the conservative buying public liked it, attracted by the price (only £5 more than the Tiger 90) and, paradoxically, the fact that it looked very much like a single. Whether intentional or not, Turner's characteristically compact design resulted in an engine that was no wider than a contemporary single, and from certain angles even looked like one. Part of this was necessity: in order to get the Speed Twin into production as quickly and as cheaply as possible, it used the Tiger 90 chassis and 63mm x 80mm bore and stroke from the Tiger 70 single. The initial idea for an overhead-cam twin was rejected on cost grounds, but the basic layout of the Triumph twin was born. It was a 360-

degree vertical twin with big central flywheel, two high, gear-driven camshafts, plunger oil pump and cast-iron barrel. So although Turner's twin was a new concept, there was much about it that was very familiar to a whole generation of riders, which lessened its revolutionary impact and paved the way for its acceptance. What also helped were the clean, symmetrical looks with the classy Aramanth Red finish, plus chrome highlights. Knowingly or not, Edward Turner had established a 'Triumph look' that was to stand the company in good stead for the next 30 years.

It was an instant success, and the company followed it in 1938 with the more sporting Tiger 100, which really did have 100mph potential. Unfortunately, its 33bhp also proved too much for the basic engine, and snapped con-rods and broken cranks were not uncommon until the company got to grips with the problems.

War interrupted Triumph's new-found success, though it is instructive to know that BSA was aiming to introduce a rival 500cc (30.5cu in) twin in 1940, which

showed just how far Triumph had leapt ahead of its rivals. For the moment, though, the Speed Twin had to give way to a 350cc (21cu in) version, the 3TW, which needed some adaptation for army use, plus the 3SW and 3HW 350 singles (sidevalve

BELOW: A 1975 Triumph Trident T160

The 1952 Triumph Thunderbird 650 was produced in response to demand from the American market

ABOVE: Neat and clean, the TZ1350 introduced unit-construction

and ohv, respectively). But Bettmann and Schulte's factory in Priory Street was destroyed in the Coventry blitz in November 1940. As a temporary measure, the works were moved to some unused buildings in Warwick (an ex-Methodist chapel held the design team) before an all-new factory was built at Meriden, a village just a few miles south-west of Coventry. Meriden became synonymous with Triumph, and the company benefited from this green-field site and very quickly had production up and running again. But as Triumph grew after the war, the Meriden factory had to be expanded again and again. Although Triumph is often seen as the archetype of all that was wrong with the old-school British motorcycle industry, it mustn't be forgotten that in the two decades after the war it was a tremendous success story, producing thousands of bikes a year, and profitably too. Much of the

success was down to simplicity of production, with Turner determined to streamline Triumph's production to twins only, and promote the popularity of the Meriden bikes in North America. By the late sixties, over 90 per cent of production was exported.

In fact, it was demand from the U.S.A. that encouraged Triumph's first big model launch after the war. It was a market demanding more performance, and Triumph responded with the 649cc (40cu in) Thunderbird in 1949. Again, it stole a march on the opposition, which had only recently come up with its own 500 twins. The 650 produced little more power than the Tiger 100 (34bhp) but it was in a more relaxed way, and was not lacking in stamina. In a superb piece of public relations, three Thunderbirds were raced around the Montlhéry race track in northern France for 500 miles at an average

148km/h (92mph) with a final flying lap of 100. (No one, of course, mentioned the 'practice' run shortly before, where a crankcase was holed.)

The Thunderbirds continued the same Triumph look established by the Speed Twin, with the addition of the headlamp nacelle, which greatly tidied up the handlebar area. It spread to the rest of the range, and lasted right through the fifties. The nacelle was really a forerunner of the brief vogue for bodywork in the 1950s; perhaps it was the scooter influence that encouraged Triumph to half-enclose the rear wheel in what became known as the 'Bathtub' (because it looked like one). The aim was to make motorcycling a cleaner

and more civilized activity, which was laudable enough, but an increasingly sports-obsessed market derided this excess metal which often found itself relegated to the back of the garage.

A more enduring model was the TR5 Trophy, a dual-purpose on/off-road bike that used an all-alloy version of the twin. This alloy engine had an interesting history, with its origins in war surplus generator units which allowed post-war racers a better-cooled Triumph twin. Meriden's experimental department got to work on one (unofficially, as Edward Turner saw most racing as a waste of money) and with twin carburettors, power was up to 47bhp at 7,000rpm. Ernie Lyons

BELOW: The 1981 Thunderbird revived the old name for a year or two

33

To cut costs, the 1967 Tiger Cub now shared parts with the BSA Bantam

won the 1946 Manx Grand Prix on one (despite breaking the bike's downtubes on the fifth lap). In the face of such success, Turner relented, and GP replicas were offered. The TR5 was a successful competitor in the ISDT but, being sold with lights, was a genuine dual-purpose bike.

Meanwhile, despite Edward Turner's post-war determination to build only twins, he could not ignore the rapidly growing market for lightweight bikes and scooters. Triumph's answer came in 1953 with the

149cc (9cu in) Terrier. Billed as a 'Real Triumph in Miniature', it certainly looked that way, with its headlamp nacelle and familiar tank badge. The ohv single itself was of unit-construction with a four-speed gearbox and, although it suffered from teething troubles (which went on longer than such troubles should), it developed into a highly popular bike for learners. The Terrier was joined by the 199cc (12cu in) Tiger Cub in 1954 and over 100,000 were made before it was finally dropped in the

late sixties, by which time it had been far outclassed by the faster, stronger Japanese opposition. But the Tiger Cub was only part of Triumph's answer to the imports. By now taken over by BSA (though a smaller company than the BSA conglomerate, Triumph sold more bikes), it unveiled the Triumph Tigress scooters (also sold as the BSA Sunbeam). Designed by Turner, these were offered in a choice of a 175cc (11cu in) BSA Bantam-powered version, or a 250cc (15cu in) four-stroke twin. The

250, in particular, was fast but lacked a Vespa's convenience and style. In any case, the scooter boom had passed its peak when the Tigress appeared in 1959, and sales were disappointing.

The Bonneville

Triumph had happier experiences with bigger bikes. American dealers were complaining that even the Thunderbird now wasn't fast enough, and in 1954 the T110 gave them their answer. As well as bigger valves and higher compression, it had a swinging-arm rear suspension, alternator electrics and improved braking. It could also manage 183km/h (114mph), according to contemporary road tests, and Johnny Allen took a tuned T110 in a cigar-shaped shell to 214mph on Bonneville salt flats, Utah. It was a new world speed record for motorcycles.

Allen's record was to lend its name to perhaps the most famous Triumph of all – the Bonneville. This was really no more nor less than a tuned, twin-carburettor T110 but somehow, as the fastest machine of its type (and from the early 1960s, with good handling as well), it captured the public's imagination. Although unable to achieve the 120mph its T120 name implied, it was still faster than most things on the road as well as being reasonably tractable and easy to ride through town. The Bonnie was the Honda FireBlade of its day and as the decade progressed it was modernized in some ways, acquiring unit-construction in 1963 and 12-volt electrics shortly afterwards. But as the horsepower race continued, so did the pressure to increase power year on year, from what was now an elderly basic design. Certainly

The T160 Trident offered electric start and a five-speed gearbox, but still didn't manage to save the company

Meriden managed to squeeze out a little more power each year, but the price to be paid soon became evident in increased vibration and reduced tractability. In a futile attempt to keep ahead of the growing Japanese opposition, the Bonneville was becoming overtuned. On the other hand, many believed the very last 'real' Bonnevilles of 1969/70 represented the peak of the bike's career, with a heavier flywheel to partially quell the vibration and various measures taken to combat oil leaks.

Still, others thought that the single-carburettor TR6 650 was a much nicer machine, being nearly as fast without being overstressed. It was the TR6 that became a police force favourite as the Triumph Saint, which allegedly stood for **S**top **A**nything **I**n **N**o **T**ime!

With all this emphasis on the big twins, it might be thought that Triumph was forgetting its roots, but in 1957 a small twin arrived with very different priorities. The 3TA was an up-to-date (at the time)

350cc (21cu in) unit-construction machine, aimed as much at America as the U.K. where 250s were thought too small, even for learners. In layout, it followed the familiar Turner vertical-twin pattern, with two high-mounted camshafts and hemispherical combustion chambers, the real change being to unit-construction of the gearbox with the engine, which made for a more rigid structure. Incidentally, the 3TA was also known as the '21', both because 350cc equalled 21 cubic inches

(more familiar to Americans) and the year 1957 marked the 21st anniversary of the Triumph Engineering Company. The 3TA was relatively light so that its 18.5bhp was enough for 129km/h (80mph), easy to ride and very economical. In short, the 3TA was also a return to the less stressed Speed Twin days. Its safe-and-sensible ethos was marked by the peak of Edward Turner's enclosure period, with optional leg guards and screen to make a practical, all-year-round motorcycle. Of course, as noted above, that wasn't what the growing youth market required, a fact which Triumph's smaller twins were soon to reflect.

A 500cc (31cu in) version soon followed in 1959, using the same 65.5mm stroke as the 350, which meant it actually had oversquare (69mm x 65.5mm) dimensions. No doubt Bert Hopwood (by then in a senior position at Meriden) had a hand in this, as he had long been keen on a modular range where different bikes shared the same components, thus saving costs and simplifying spares supply. Still, the new 500 showed no signs of being compromised; it was a likeable, free-revving bike, with significantly more power than the 3TA but little more weight. The 5TA Speed Twin produced 27bhp at 6,500rpm and, like the 350, had the rear panelling as standard. Inevitably, sports versions soon followed. First was the T100A Tiger in 1960 which used a 9:1 compression and different camshafts for 32bhp at 7,000rpm. It also had Energy Transfer ignition, which allowed a quick conversion to running without battery or lights. This was for competition, where the smaller Triumph twins were building up a good record in trials and the ISDT, while the 650s were out track racing.

Bonnie's final years: the 1981 T140 (ABOVE) and (BELOW) the 1977 Silver Jubilee

A whole range of 350s and 500s was to follow through the sixties, underlining the fact that Triumph twins outsold their rival BSAs by five to one. This created tensions in the BSA-Triumph amalgamation in that Triumph was ostensibly the junior partner while being more successful in the motorcycle market. (BSA, of course, was a huge company with many more strings to its bow than motorcycles, but tension existed just the same.) So 1962 saw another sports 500, the T100SS which used 650 influence to produce 34bhp at 7,000rpm, while the following year there was a sporting 350 (marking the return of the Tiger 90 name) with 27bhp at 7,500rpm. The ultimate small twin (in terms of power) was the Daytona of 1967 which used twin carburettors, bigger valves and a high compression of 9.75:1 (these were the days of high-octane five-star petrol). The Daytona could manage 182km/h (113mph) from its 39bhp at 7,400rpm, though like the Bonneville was showing signs of being overtuned. Also like the Bonnie, it was named after an American sporting achievement. A works 500 won the Daytona Production Race in 1967 when Doug Hele's attention had boosted the bike's power to 50bhp at 8,800rpm. Meanwhile, Bonnevilles were doing well in production racing at home with victories in the Production TT in 1967 and '69, while Bonnies filled five of the first seven places in the 1969 Thruxton 500 and also won the Barcelona 24-hour race that year.

The Triple
However fast the racing Bonnevilles were, a new breed of bike was about to overtake them. Bert Hopwood and Doug Hele had worked together on a 750cc (46cu in) triple as early as 1963, and even had a running prototype on the road the following year. But Triumph's board failed to share their enthusiasm, and it only got the go-ahead once they learned of Honda's imminent four-cylinder CB750. Even then, it was another two years before the new Trident (also sold in virtually identical BSA Rocket Three form) actually went on sale. Much of this was down to the infamous Umberslade Hall, BSA/Triumph's massive design centre that consumed much but produced little. Umberslade (nicknamed Slumberglade) restyled the Trident, but in a way that actually lost them buyers, so it didn't reach the market until September 1968, the same year as Honda's CB750. It was tragic that a bike that could have gone on sale at least two years earlier was inevitably compared to the CB750, which offered electric start, overhead camshaft and front disc brake, yet at no greater cost.

Still, the Trident certainly made an impact. It was one of the new breed of superbikes, and testers wrote breathlessly of 80mph in second, 110 in third and having to hang on desperately as this 'big, fast groundshaker of a machine' (*Cycle World*) leapt forward. Compared to the twins that everyone was familiar with, the Trident came over as incredibly fast, very smooth and revvy, if a little heavy as well (which it was, at 212kg/468lb). Fifty-eight bhp doesn't sound much now, but in 1969 it made the Trident one of the fastest bikes one could buy. It made a successful racer too, albeit in modified form, coming just in time to take over from the Bonneville; in 1971, Tridents won the Bol d'Or, both Production and F750TTs and scored a 1-2-3 at Daytona. It was a brief blaze of glory,

The Tiger Cub's characteristic low weight and four-stroke power made it a popular basis for a trials bike

Triumph would do anything for publicity. Here are 807 Squadron R.N.A.S. and a fleet of Triumph Tigress scooters

were a less than total success, another of the problems being 34-inch seat height! It was also planned to launch an all-new dohc 350cc twin at the same time – the Triumph Bandit. This actually got quite close to production, and several prototypes were built and tested, but the BSA/Triumph group's parlous financial state put paid to it.

Much of the company's problems stemmed from over-dependence on the huge American market with its short selling season. U.S. dealers had pressurized Triumph to produce the 650cc (40cu in) twin, then the Bonneville. Now they insisted on a 750cc version of the twin. There was some resistance at Meriden, where they knew that yet another capacity increase was too much to ask of the venerable vertical twin. But in the end they relented, and the Bonneville 750 was launched in late 1972. In practice, it was no faster than the 650 (prototypes had to be detuned when it was found that crankshafts were breaking on a regular basis), but the vibration (as the Meriden men could have told them) was worse. It has to be said that the 750's *raison d'être* was more a marketing exercise than any real advantage, though it did bring a five-speed gearbox and front disc brake as well. The company's fortunes continued down the slippery slope, with many redundancies at the BSA end, and although Lord Shawcross (brought in as a caretaker chairman) had managed to reduce the deficit, he was forced to approach the Government for financial aid. Finance was agreed with the proviso of a merger with Norton to form Norton Villiers Triumph (NVT). After some wrangling, this went ahead, but it soon became clear that Norton, under Dennis Poore, was to be the

though impressive nonetheless, and of course one particular Trident (nicknamed 'Slippery Sam' after a mid-race oil leak) won the Production TT five times. It was quite an achievement for a bike that owed much to the elderly twins and was originally intended as a stopgap.

There were a few changes in its six-year life. The Umberslade slab-side styling was soon dropped (for the U.S. market) in favour of a more traditional look, while 1973 saw a front disc brake and five-speed gearbox. There was also the X-75 Hurricane, with transformed styling by American Craig Vetter. Finally, the T160 of 1974 was NVT's last gasp with the Trident. It actually included over 200 changes from the old bike, including an electric start, and longer, lower styling and some think it was the best-looking Trident of all. Sadly, a

price of £1,215 was too much to ask (£200 more than the CB750), and the Trident's brief, but glorious career was soon over.

Meanwhile, twins were still the mainstay of Meriden's production, and it was the final 750cc version which was to keep the factory going right up to the end in 1983. The 650s had been substantially updated in 1971, shoehorned into the new oil-in-frame cycle parts, which themselves senior partner; one of Poore's first actions was to announce the closure of Meriden. However, Triumph's factory was probably the most cohesive of all the British plants, and the workforce promptly staged a sit-in, which was to last 18 months. It wasn't until early 1975 that a settlement was finally reached whereby Meriden was able to go it alone as a workers' co-operative, and probably the most famed in Britain!

At first, the 750cc twin was its sole product, in single carburettor Tiger twin-carb Bonneville form (in practice the Tiger was almost as fast, and probably pleasanter to ride as well), but a number of variants on the same theme were to follow over the years. The Meriden co-op's real problem

BELOW: Tigress missed the scooter boom

ABOVE: An odd, articulated Tina-based one-off

was that it was always short of cash, there never being enough to develop the all-new machine it needed, so the Bonneville had to struggle on. For all that, it sold in respectable numbers in the late 1970s. Although out of the performance game, it was still well liked in both Britain and the United States, and was actually the best-selling 750 in Britain for a while. There were all sorts of special editions to keep

interest alive, as well as some more fundamental changes. An electric start arrived in 1980, and there was the Tiger Trail dual-purpose version. More ambitious was the eight-valve TSS of 1982 and the 'AV' (Anti-Vibration) frame. Alas, teething troubles and Meriden's endemic problems put paid to both of them. A happier swan-song was the TR65 Thunderbird, a short-stroke, cut-price 650 which was smooth

T150 was a stunning performer, but should have been launched several years earlier

ABOVE: The Trident's three-cylinder engine owed much to Triumph twins

ABOVE: The Craig Vetter-styled Hurricane showed just how important the U.S.A. was to Triumph

and free-revving compared to the 750. And there were plans for the future when, at the 1983 Motorcycle Show in Birmingham, Triumph exhibited a new 600cc (37cu in) version of the twin, plus the prototype T2000 Phoenix. The latter was a 900cc (55cu in) liquid-cooled twin which Triumph hoped would take it to the end of the century. Sadly, none of this was to happen and the co-operative, which had struggled on for nearly ten years, finally went into liquidation in August 1983.

There is, however, a postscript. Millionaire John Bloor, who had made his fortune from house building, bought the Triumph name and sold a five-year rights deal to former spares maker Les Harris. The Harris Bonnevilles, as they became known, went into production in a south

Devon factory, and were built until 1988. So this was not the end of the Triumph story. In fact, it was the prelude to a new chapter.

Hinckley

In the 1990s, 'Hinckley' was to become as much a byword for Triumph as Meriden had been. In a way that would have seemed unbelievable not so long ago, John Bloor funded the development of a range of all-new, thoroughly modern British motorcycles. He built a factory to make them, launched them on time and to media acclaim, and has gone on selling them ever since.

When Meriden collapsed in 1983, many thought this would be the final end of the British motorcycle industry. The

difference between the new Triumph and the earlier attempts to revive the British industry (which had been labelled as such by an over-eager motorcycle press) was proper funding by a sole backer. This time, there would be no shareholders pressing for short-term profits, and no scratching around for money.

So it wasn't until early 1990, after six years of development, that the new range of Triumphs was announced. The press loved them and everyone seemed genuinely surprised (and perhaps a little relieved) that this time a British motorcycle maker had got it right first time. The new range was a whole family of bikes sharing the same steel spine frame chassis and three- or four-cylinder liquid-cooled engines of 750–1200cc (46–73cu in). It was really

ABOVE: Meanwhile, older twins were competing in classic events

OPPOSITE: The 1994 Daytona 900 was still a little too tall and heavy to be a sportster

ABOVE: 1997 Thunderbird Sport

Bert Hopwood's modular philosophy put into practice at last; the new family shared many components and allowed Triumph to launch a complete range of big bikes at one go and at a relatively low price.

There were the basic unfaired 750 and 900cc three-cylinder Tridents (John Bloor knew the value of these old-established names); 750-3 and 1000-4 Daytona sports versions; and the Trophy sports tourers, with 900-3 or 1200-4 engines. The 900cc triple seemed to be most testers' favourite, with a distinctive howling exhaust note and plenty of torque, and it seemed that the new Triumphs had character as well. Even more surprising, there were no horror stories; these Triumphs were at least as dependable as the Japanese competition.

Variations on the theme soon appeared. The Speed Triple was really the later

Daytona 900 without its fairing, and a lighter, more powerful Daytona Super III sought to catch the Japanese race replicas (though it wasn't fast or light enough). A bigger change was the Tiger 900, basically the now familiar 900 triple dressed up in off-road clothing. It followed the style of big 'dual purpose' bikes like the BMW GS, though was even less likely to get its tyres muddy.

More of a pointer to the future was the return of the Thunderbird name in late 1994, designed to spearhead a return to the American market. It was an unashamedly nostalgic machine, with old-style Triumph tank, badge and silencers, more chrome and spoked wheels. It also (to sighs of relief from the shorter-legged) had a lower seat height than the other Hinckley Triumphs. The 900cc triple

OPPOSITE: The 1997 Daytona T595 was the fastest Hinckley Triumph yet

ABOVE: An early Trident 900

was detuned to suit the character of this retro cruiser (a real growth market in the nineties) though a sharper Thunderbird Sport was to appear in 1997.

More significant that year was the launch of the substantially new Daytona T595. If any of the new Triumphs had lagged behind the opposition, it was the supposedly sporting Daytonas, which were really too tall and heavy to compete. The new bike cured that with an alloy frame, far more nimble handling and a new fuel-injected 955cc (58cu in) version of the triple, with 130bhp and a top speed of around 257km/h (160mph). It was a success, and soon became Triumph's best-selling bike. At the other end of the scale, the Trophies moved further towards being true tourers (though their lack of shaft-drive was a bar to success). The T595 was followed in late 1998 by a sports touring

version, the Sprint ST, which was substantially all-new. (It wasn't before time, as eight years on, the original spine frame was starting to look very dated indeed.) Moreover, riders of early STs found them smooth, civilized and deceptively fast. Triumph was back.

TRIUMPH *Germany 1903–57*
This was a subsidiary of the better-known English Triumph, which split from Coventry in 1930. Until then, it built own versions of Coventry bikes, afterwards developing its own two-strokes to 350cc and used Sachs and MAG engines. It resumed production in 1948 with a range of utility two-stroke split-singles of 125–350cc (8–21cu in), powering lightweights and the 200cc (12cu in) Contessa scooter. The company was taken over by Grundig in 1957.

TRIUMPH *U.S.A. 1912*
A subsidiary of the English Triumph, building singles from imported parts.

TROPFEN *Germany 1923–24*
Another attempt (there were a few) by an airship maker to attempt a motorcycle with airship-like full enclosure on a 248/308cc (15/19cu in) two-stroke.

TRUMP (TRUMP-JAP) *England 1906–23*
Utilized a full range of JAP engines of 248–996cc (15–61cu in), as well as the British-Anzani V-twin and 269cc (16cu in) Peco two-stroke.

TSUBASA *Japan 1955–60*
Own 246/345cc (15/21cu in) ohv singles, later a 125cc (8cu in) two-stroke.

TÜRKHEIMER *Italy 1902–05*
There were 1.25hp lightweights from this motorcycle importer.

TVS *India 1976–*
Produced licence-built Batavus mopeds, then entered a licencing agreement with Suzuki in the 1980s. Produced its own 60cc/3.7cu inch scooter (the Scooty) from 1993 and is now the Indian market leader in mopeds.

TX *Germany 1924–26*
Had an unusual frame using the big top tube as a fuel tank. Powered by 132/174cc (8/11cu in) Bekamo two-strokes.

TYLER *England 1913–23*
Made lightweights powered by four-stroke Precision and two-stroke Villiers or in-house engines.

TYPHOON *Sweden 1949–51*
An advanced 198cc (12cu in) two-stroke.

TYPHOON *The Netherlands 1952–68*
Concentrated on mopeds, later importing the Italian Giulietta moped under its own name.

U

UDE *Germany 1924–25*
A 249cc (15cu in) three-port two-stroke.

ULTIMA *France 1908–58*
Used bought-in engines from Aubier-Dunne, JAP and Zurcher, among others. Like most French and German factories, it concentrated on small two-strokes after 1945.

UNIBUS *England 1920–22*
A fully enclosed scooter with leaf-sprung suspension, a 269cc (16cu in) two-stroke and 16-inch wheels.

UNION *Sweden 1943–52*
Only used JAP ohv singles, from 348–498cc (21–30cu in).

UNIVERSAL *Switzerland 1928–64*
Used bought-in engines from a variety of suppliers, including Ilo, JAP and Anzani, but also built its own 676/990cc (41/60cu in) sv V-twins for the Swiss Army. After 1945, went on making in-house engines, notably a 578cc (35cu in) flat twin and a 248cc (15cu in) single, both with unit-construction and shaft-drive.

UNIVERSELLE *Germany 1925–29*
Ioe four-stroke singles of 183–247cc (11–15cu in), with unit-construction.

ABOVE: The Ural Cossack 650D, of which not many were exported

ABOVE: The Jupiter 350 was another product of the former U.S.S.R.

BELOW: To Western eyes, the Ural simply looked odd

URAL *Former U.S.S.R. 1945–*
Ural was a product of the Soviet Union's pragmatic if ruthless post-war policy of seizing any valuable plant in occupied Germany and taking it back to the Motherland. So it was with BMW's production equipment which was transferred from the Eisenach factory into Russia. There, the flat twin was faithfully reproduced, and was even passed on (third-hand, you might say) to China.

Several factories in the U.S.S.R. built the ex-BMW, but the Kiev, Irbit, Cossack, Dneiper and Neval were all basically the same machine. It first surfaced as the Ural Mars M63 (even retaining a BMW model name) and turned out to be a combination of an R66 and wartime R75. There were

updates from time to time, notably swinging-arm suspension and a capacity increase to 650cc (40cu in), but there was much of the original still in place. Even the R75's driven sidecar wheel and auxiliary gearchange were retained which, according to the maker, made gearchanging easier when towing a plough!

URANIA *Germany 1934–39*
Made Sachs and Ilo-engined two-strokes to 123cc (7.5cu in).

UT *Germany 1922–59*
Used many different bought-in engines prior to 1939 (Bekamo, Blackburne, JAP, Küchen and Bark) but concentrated on Sachs and Ilo-engined lightweights after the war.

UTILIA *France 1929–36*
A large variety of engines were used, from 98cc (6cu in) two-strokes to 498cc (30cu in) four-strokes, all bought-in.

V

VAGA *Italy 1925–35*
Produced 124cc (8cu in) two-strokes initially, followed by bought-in four-strokes including units from JAP and Sturmey-Archer.

VAL *England 1913–24*
Used JAP sv singles of 488cc (30cu in).

VALIANT *U.S.A. c.1964–65*
Made a 197cc (12cu in) Villiers-engined version of the Simplex minibike.

VAN VEEN *Germany 1978–81*
Henk van Veen distributed Kreider mopeds in Holland, but is best known for his rotary-engined OCR1000. The heavy 295kg (650lb) machine used a water-cooled Wankel engine and shaft-drive. Claimed top speed was 150mph. Limited numbers made.

VAP *France 1951–early 1970s*
Built moped engines, later complete lightweights.

VAREL *Germany 1952–53*
Produced 43cc (2.6cu in) mopeds and 99cc (6cu in) Moto-engined scooters.

VASCO *England 1921–23*
Used 261cc (16cu in) Orbit power, then 349cc (21cu in) Broler two-stroke singles.

VASSENA *Italy 1926–29*
A 124cc (8cu in) two-stroke with horizontal cylinder.

VATERLAND *Germany 1933–39*
Sachs-engined lightweights of 98 and 120cc (6 and 7.3cu in).

VECCHIETTI *Italy 1954–57*
Mopeds using 49cc (3cu in) Victoria engines.

VELAMOS *Czechoslovakia 1927–30*
Used its own three-port two-strokes of 246–496cc (15–30cu in), designed by Gustav Heinz.

VELOCETTE *England 1904–71*
From the beginning and right to the end,

Velocette was a family concern and three generations of the Goodman family ran it: John Goodman set the firm up, his sons Percy and Eugene (both talented engineers) took care of it between the wars, while their sister Ethel acted as buyer and her husband, George Denly, was sales manager. In the last 20 years, *their* sons Bertie and Peter took charge of the company.

Although such continuity was one of Velocette's strengths, it is arguable that it also held the seeds of its destruction, for while Percy Goodman was interested in building racing singles, his brother Eugene was set on that other, probably more elusive goal – the practical motorcycle for the man in the street. There is no evidence of any friction between the two brothers as

The rotary-engined Van Veen was only made in small numbers

The all-French Velo-Solex is now made in Hungary

a result of their conflicting interests, but it did mean that the small firm's resources (Velocette never employed more than 400 people) were often over-stretched by ambitious new projects it could ill afford.

Being so small, Velocette could not afford to mass-produce its utility bikes, so these cost more than they should have done, and none was successful. In fact, when the company was wound up, it cited the Viceroy scooter as instrumental in its downfall. On the other hand, Veloce Ltd. had a talent for sporting four-stroke singles, and its high quality, high performance 350s and 500s, in their classic black and gold livery, are seen by many as the definitive British singles.

John Goodman began life in Germany as Johannes Gujtemann, but anglicized his name when he emigrated to England. His fledgling company experimented in all sorts of fields, including roller skates, a car, and even rickshaws, until the success of an advanced little 276cc (17cu in) unit-construction bike and a more conventional 500cc (30.5cu in) machine convinced him that this was the way to go. There were 250cc two-stroke 'Velocettes' (the name stuck) from 1913, which helped give the company a firmer footing.

Percy and Eugene soon proved themselves fine design engineers, and it was the former who succeeded, where established companies like Sunbeam and Norton were still struggling, in designing a reliable overhead-camshaft racing single. Using an early strobe light in the early 1920s, Percy discovered the correct cam profiles to use, and also solved the problem of lubrication. The result was the 350cc (21cu in) K-series racer which won the

ABOVE and BELOW: Classic Velocette singles, of which the 1934 KSS (above) was one, formed the basis of the company's reputation

Junior TT in 1926. Suddenly, Velocette was high-profile, and orders flowed in so fast that it was forced to move to a larger factory. More TT successes followed, aided by the first production foot gearchange, with a positive stop lever. (Every manual-transmission motorcycle uses this now, but Velocette was first.) Another Velocette first was the combined dual seat, and that too was soon adopted by everyone else. Both of these stemmed from a designer named Harold Willis, who was prolific in his inventiveness and responsible for many of Velocette's innovations.

Although, by 1930, Velocette's main production consisted of the road- and race-going K-series (with the lovely black and gold finish already a feature), Eugene was keen to produce a cheaper bike which would appeal to non-enthusiasts which, after all, had been the Velocette's original intention. The result was the GTP250, a two-stroke single in the now traditional black and gold, in addition to a few innovations of its own, notably the use of the engine as a stress-bearing member of the chassis, and coil ignition. A throttle-controlled oil pump was added in another few years. But like the more glamorous Velocettes, the GTP was built up to a standard of quality, rather than down to a price.

Meanwhile, that very philosphy was undermining the K-series. Popular as it was, the ohc single needed skilful assembly (especially the cam's bevel-drive). Eugene came up with the answer, and it was to prove Velocette's mainstay for the rest of the firm's life. The overhead camshaft was too expensive, but a conventional ohv set-up, with long, whippy pushrods would limit near-80mph top speed little lower than that of the K-series. It also introduced automatic ignition control in 1936 – yet another Velocette first. The M-series bikes were not perfect: they could leak oil, used Velocette's unusual single plate clutch and it needed a knack to start them. But it sold well, and kept the company profitable right through to the mid-1950s.

Supercharged

The very inventiveness that produced Velocette's many firsts also led to other projects that failed to make it. There were various attempts at twin overhead camshafts, and Harold Willis experimented with rotary valves, while Phil Irving (on a brief sojourn away from Vincent) designed a 600cc (37cu in) vertical twin with shaft-drive and rear suspension. More promising was the famous 'Roarer', a supercharged 500cc twin-cylinder racer. It was certainly advanced for its time, being rear-sprung, shaft-driven and with full-width hubs. Unfortunately, it was only once run competitively, in the 1938 TT, when Stanley Woods failed to make much of an impression with it (though he won the Junior TT on a 350 single and was second in the Senior). After the war, the FIM's ban on supercharged racers was enough to put paid to the project.

Unlike the larger British factories, Velocette did not produce endless ranks of motorcycles for wartime despatch riders, lacking the mass-production facilities to do so, and although there was a military-specification MAF, most of the company's wartime work was in the form of sub-contracts for such things as gun components. But even while war was still

The 1935 GTP250 was an attempt to reach the ride-to-work market

engine revs and thus power. His solution was to mount the camshaft high up (driven by intermediate gears), which allowed the use of relatively short, stiff pushrods, not quite as powerful as the K-series, but not far off, and much easier and cheaper to build. Ironically enough, although cost was the new M-series' *raison d'être*, its advantage was severely compromised by

the use of costly helical teeth for the timing gears. Once again, Velocette had chosen the fundamentally correct engineering solution with little heed to the expense.

In production form, the first M-series was the 250cc (15cu in) MOV of 1933. At around 97km/h (60mph), it was fast for its capacity, sweet and relatively smooth, no doubt helped by the almost square cylinder

dimensions of 68mm x 68.25mm. The following year, a longer-stroke 350cc (21cu in) version, the MAC, was unveiled, which used the same chassis as the 250 and weighed only 4.5kg (10lb) more. It could top 121km/h (75mph) and, like the MOV, was a deserved success. The range was completed in 1935 with the 500cc (30.5cu in) MSS ('Super Sports') with a

Thruxton in a rare silver finish. Note the adjustment slot for the rear damper

being waged, Eugene Goodman's thoughts kept returning to his motorcycle for everyman – simple, reliable and well-built.

The result (also worked on by Phil Irving, and finalized by Charles Udall, who had also productionized the M-series) was the LE. It was unusual in many ways, chiefly for its flat-twin layout, shaft-drive and water-cooling. A prototype of the 150cc (9cu in) machine was running in 1945 but it was four years before it finally entered production. It was an ambitious project which swallowed much of Velocette's slender resources when it could have been concentrating on the popular, profitable MAC. Sadly, the LE was expensive for a utility bike, and sales were disappointing. Eugene had predicted sales of 14,500 for 1950, but in fact less than 3,000 bikes found homes. The LE was certainly quiet, docile and easy to ride, providing a measure of weather protection from its legshields, and it was very comfortable. But it was also heavy and underpowered (despite a bigger 192cc/11.7cu inch engine in 1951) and only the police really took to it. Meanwhile the 350cc MAC had been gradually updated with telescopic forks in 1948, an alloy engine in 1951 and a swinging-arm frame two years later. But like Triumph and other British manufacturers, Velocette was faced with a demand for more capacity from its American customers, and responded by bringing back the 500cc MSS in 1954. Both were updated a few years later into the 350 Viper and 500 Venom, with more racing success (Bertie Goodman was a noted rider) bolstering the Velocette heritage.

Coffin Nails

But Eugene hadn't given up on the utility end of the market, and Velocette's response to criticisms of the underpowered sidevalve LE was the overhead-valved Valiant of 1956. On paper, this seemed just the thing, with a four-speed gearbox, air-cooling to reduce weight, conventional motorcycle styling (though still with the practical shaft-drive) and twice as much power as the LE. Unfortunately, it was based on the LE's bottom-end, which couldn't cope with 12bhp, and engine failure often resulted. The Valiant remained available until 1963, by which time sales had reduced to a trickle.

But even with the Valiant, there was still time for Velocette to turn itself around. What really set the company on the slippery slope was the Viceroy scooter. Like BSA/Triumph, Velocette woke up late to the scooter boom with a bike that was too big, heavy and expensive to compete. It was yet another variation on the flat twin theme, this time a two-stroke version of the 247cc (15cu in). In theory, it handled better than a Vespa, with its tubular frame, big 12-inch wheels and good weight distribution, but it also weighed a lot more and was expensive. Once again, predictions of mass sales proved hopelessly optimistic; the aim was 5,000 in 1962, but a mere 300 had been sold when the scooter was dropped in 1964. There were other attempts to find alternative

ABOVE: The Venom Thruxton of 1965 was the final development

outlets for the LE flat twin: its quiet operation gave it potential as a stationary power plant, though that came to nothing. Instead, Velocette went ahead with the Vogue, a fully-panelled, twin-headlamped luxury commuter in the mould of the Ariel Leader. It was no match for the younger Ariel, though, and not many were sold.

While money was being spent and lost on the various lightweight projects, the Viper and Venom went on selling steadily, though even these were beginning to look increasingly outdated against home-built twins and, as the 1960s progressed, new rivals from Honda and Kawasaki. There was one final development in 1965 with the Venom Thruxton. Its inspiration was a squish-type cylinder-head produced by Velocette's U.S. importer, Lou Branch, which the factory adopted for its ultimate

big single. Around a thousand Thruxtons were built over the last few years, and one even won the first Production TT in 1967. But from that year onwards, the company was being kept afloat only by the relatively lucrative spares production for Royal Enfield, which had recently collapsed. Production gradually slowed, although one of the final contracts was for 194 500cc engines for the Italian-built Indian 500. This was the idea of American entrepreneur Floyd Clymer, who wished to sell a combination of Italian styling and British engineering. It was not a success. So Velocette finally went into liquidation in February 1971, and yet another famous British name went under. Sadly, if Velocette had concentrated on what it was good at, it might possibly have still been around today.

BELOW: A 1956 500cc (31.5cu in) Venom

VELO-SOLEX *France 1946–91*
With its 49cc (3cu in) two-stroke mounted on top of the front wheel the bike, like the Citroën 2cv, was part of the French landscape, and no French rural family would have been complete without one. It was really a cross between a clip-on engine and a conventional moped. Taken over by Motobécane in 1974, it is now made in Hungary. To date, over 6 million have been produced.

VELOX *Czechoslovakia 1923–26*
First used a 147cc (9cu in) Villiers, later 123/147cc (7.5/9cu in) Bekamo two-strokes.

VENUS *England 1920–22*
Used a 318cc (19.4cu in) Dalm engine.

VENUS *Germany 1920–22*
A Sachs-engined scooter of 98–174cc (6–11cu in).

VERGA *Italy 1951–54*
A 73cc (4.5cu in) two-stroke, with swinging-arm rear suspension.

VERLOR *France 1930–38*
Produced 98–120cc (6–7.3cu in) lightweights with Aubier-Dunne or Stainless engines.

VEROS *Italy 1922–24*
A rebadged Verus (see below) for export to Italy.

VERUS *England 1919–25*
Choice of own two-strokes to 269cc (16cu in) or larger Blackburne four-strokes.

VESPA
See Piaggio.

VESUV *Germany 1924–26*
Own 246cc (15cu in) two-stroke in step-through frame.

VIATKA *Russia 1957–79*
Copy of the Vespa scooter in 150/175cc (9/11cu in) versions.

VIBERTI *Italy 1955–late 1960s*
Produced mopeds and 123cc (7.5cu in) lightweights.

VICTA *England 1912–13*
Used a Precision 499cc (30cu in) single.

VICTORIA *Scotland 1902–26*
No connection with the German Victoria, it used a variety of bought-in engines from 127–688cc (8–42cu in). Built in Glasgow.

VICTORIA *Germany 1899–1966*
Founded in 1886 and originally a bicycle maker, it built a prototype motorcycle in 1899 but it was another six years before full production of Zedel and Fafnir-engined machines appeared. After World War I it briefly used BMW's fore-aft flat twin before designing its own, and introduced a new range of singles in 1928 with bought-in engines (the 198–499cc/12–30cu inch Horex and the licence-built Sturmey-Archer). After 1945, it initially produced clip-ons only, then two-strokes up to 247cc (15cu in). Attempted to return upmarket with the shaft-driven 347cc (21cu in) V-twin Bergmeister in 1951, but a falling market caused it to concentrate on lightweights only, some with Italian Parilla engines. Merged with DKW and Express to form Zweirad Union in 1958, and the name finally disappeared in 1966.

ABOVE: 1938 Victoria Aero 250cc (15cu in)

BELOW and OPPOSITE: 1954 Victoria Bergmeister 350cc (21cu in)

ABOVE: Sales brochure for the Victory. Inspired by Harley-Davidson's success, Polaris designed and built an all-new rival

VICTORY *Italy 1950–55*
Made Villiers-engined lightweights of 98–123cc (6–7.5cu in).

VICTORY *U.S.A. 1998–*
The 1990s have seen the revival or rebirth of some very famous marques, names such as Ducati, spurred on by racing success and American corporate finance; Triumph rescued by a self-made millionaire; Laverda promising a new three-cylinder bike in the near future. It is part of a general revival of interest in the European industry that is now managing to flourish alongside the Japanese giants. At the time of writing, there is even an all-new marque

from France, the Voxan. And let's not forget the non-Japanese manufacturer whose revival began years ago – Harley-Davidson. In little more than a decade, Harley transformed itself from corporate no-hoper to an all-American success story. So successful, that other American entrepreneurs have sat up and taken notice of this newly-profitable field of operation.

One of them was Polaris. Based in Wisconsin, it makes golf carts, ATVs and jet-skis. Always on the look-out for new opportunities, it had noted Harley's success, as well as its inability to keep up with demand. Not only that, but sales in the cruiser market sector were high and

profit margins generous. It was also a sector where being an American manufacturer was a positive bonus. A survey discovered that many existing Polaris customers already rode bikes so, for a manufacturer like Polaris, it was a golden marketing opportunity. Consequently, in 1993 the big decision was made to proceed.

The first thing to do was to go out and buy a Harley (an FXRS), plus a Honda Shadow. Each was stripped down and painstakingly costed, part by part, the aim being to determine which components Polaris should make in-house and which should be bought-in. It was decided early

on that the V-twin engine (could it really have been anything else?) would have to be made in-house, to give the project credibility. Harley sold on being a genuine all-American motorcycle, and the Polaris could not afford to be anything else.

With the best will in the world, the Polaris design team had little experience of designing bikes, so it sensibly bought up most of the competition, the Honda Valkyrie, Harley Road King – even non-cruisers such as Ducati's Monster, and evaluated all in great detail. Everyone liked the Kawasaki Vulcan V-twin (then the biggest, at 1470cc/90cu inches) so Polaris determined to build something slightly

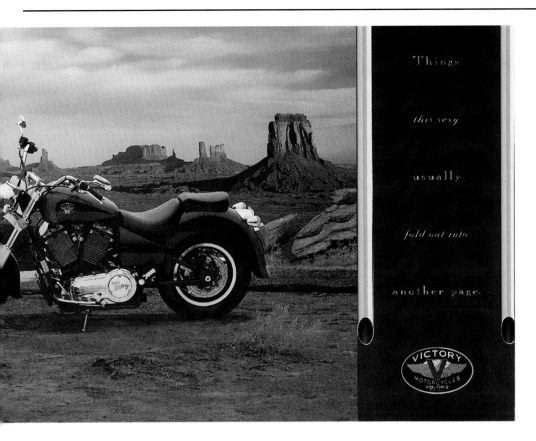

Things

this sexy

usually

fold out into

another page.

bigger still. It came out at 1507cc (92cu in) and three years on, as this is written, Yamaha has just launched a 1600cc (98cu in) twin. It may be that once this book is published, on the shelves and you are reading it, Polaris or someone else will have come up with something bigger still. One thing that emerged during the evaluation rides was that many of the cruisers had unpleasant, wallowy handling when pressed hard. It's often argued that for the laid-back riding style that cruisers are supposed to provide, this doesn't really matter, but the Polaris team was apparently determined to produce a cruiser that handled well at speed as well as when cruising.

Geoff Burgess was brought in as project leader. A Scotsman by birth, he had worked for Norton-Villiers in the mid-1960s before emigrating to North America and eventually joining Polaris to develop the Victory into a production bike. A 'mule' rolling chassis was built on which critical factors like wheelbase, rake and trail were adjustable. 'Francis' (as it was called) was taken out on the road, and everything was adjusted until it was deemed to be just so. Polaris' own engine wasn't ready at this stage, so Francis was powered by a Harley Sportster engine, which had the additional benefit of being able to fool onlookers that this secret prototype was really no more than a well-

used Harley-Davidson. As the project developed, the frame's design became more of a fixed entity and in fact the engine design parameters had to be changed to get it to fit. Because (so Polaris claims) the Victory handles well with the chassis it has got, it was necessary to shorten the engine by changing the Vee angle from 55 degrees to 50, which made the engine 28mm shorter. Another case of engine-determined-by-chassis was the decision to go for a balance-shaft. It was a choice between that and rubber mounting, but to reduce flex the designers wanted to use the engine as a solidly-mounted stressed member. That, in turn, meant that they needed an alternative means of quelling vibration – hence the balance-shaft. One more apocryphal story concerning the Victory's handling development. The test riders decided something wasn't quite right, but couldn't work out what it was. Someone (history does not record who) remembered that the Norton Manx's superlative handling stemmed partly from having both wheel spindles in line with the crankshaft; so they dropped the Victory's crank by an inch, and all was apparently well.

Engine Design
In fact, the Victory's engine ended up significantly different from the original outline specification, which envisaged an air-cooled, pushrod ohv twin with rubber mounting, carburettors and no balancer shaft. The production engine uses more sophisticated technology, with fuel injection, oil cooling and overhead cams. It was an interesting departure from Harley-Davidson's philosophy of keeping its power unit deliberately low-tech.

Mark Bader joined the Polaris team in May 1995 to head engine development when some of those changes from the initial specifications were implemented. The decision to abandon pushrods was apparently an easy one as the Victory engine had a projected life of 10 to 15 years, which meant that single overhead cams had to be squeezed in without increasing the engine's height; they managed it by mounting the cams low in the cylinder heads. One area completely new to Polaris was fuel injection, so an outside supplier was brought in which also withdrew suddenly, but a replacement (MBE) was soon found.

The top end of the engine was coming together nicely, but the crankcases weren't ready, being a month behind schedule. So for bench testing, the team took a 159kg (350lb) block of aluminium, and carved it to accept the heads and barrels. Nicknamed the Hammer, it was bulky and block-like, but it served its purpose. There were undoubtedly a lot of crossed fingers on a Friday in September 1996 when the first Victory top-end was finally installed into the Hammer, everything hooked up and ready to go. The key was turned and ... it wouldn't start. They purged air from the fuel system, tried again, and the Victory V-twin roared into life for the first time.

After that first excitement, the donkey work began; fuel mapping for the injection had to be done through a long and laborious process of calculating the engine's fuel needs at every combination of speed and load. The basics were done on the bench, but final tweaks had to be made on the road. So a running Victory was hitched up to a sidecar, and Jeff Moore of MBE sat in the chair, tapping away at his laptop, which was hooked into all the engine's essential points. Geoff Burgess later recalled that the fuel mapping and fine tuning took about six months to complete. Yet more road testing ensued on what was now a pre-production prototype. As with anything all-new, the priority was to accumulate some miles in the hope that if anything broke, it would break then. All the time, work was progressing on styling details, and of course the launch.

The first public unveiling was at the Planet Hollywood restaurant in Bloomington, Minnesota in June 1997; then it was time to start the show circuit, and two Victory V92Cs, the '92' referring to the engine capacity in cubic inches, went on display at Sturgis that August. And at Daytona, a lot more people had the opportunity to ride the Victory for the first time. Among them was journalist Ian Kerr, who wrote about it for *Motorcycle Sport & Leisure*: 'The 1507cc twin certainly delivers its claimed 85lb ft of torque – open the throttle and it goes, in no uncertain terms. It's an instantaneous response too, thanks to the electronic fuel injection and engine management. Roll-on in any gear was excellent, and if you want to brave both Florida radar traps and the wind, three-figure speeds are easily obtained ...' He also remarked that it had a clunky gearchange (which would be changed for production), felt well balanced, was stable through bends, though ground clearance was inevitably compromised, and exuded quality. He was also convinced that people would be queuing up to buy it. Whether this all-new motorcycle fulfils its early promise remains to be seen, but it's a good start.

The final Vincent was the enclosed Black Prince

VILLA *Italy 1968–88*
Concentrated on two-stroke lightweights, mostly with bought-in engines, but used its own engines in successful motocross bikes. Master-minded by ex-racers, Francesco and Walter Villa.

VILLOF *Spain 1951–61*
75–123cc (4.6–7.5cu in) two-strokes, both

Hispano-Villiers-powered and with in-house engines.

VINCENT-HRD *England 1927–55*
Today, a one-litre V-twin with a cruising speed of 100mph, able to top 120 and with great attention given to rider comfort, would be a respectable sports-tourer. Little more than half a century ago, the Vincent-

HRD V-twin must have seemed like something from outer space. It was faster than any contemporary racer (let alone road bike), yet behaved like a well-mannered tourer. It had cantilevered rear suspension (25 years before most motorcycles adopted rear suspension of any type) and was built of the finest materials. It was, to put it mildly, a milestone machine.

Philip Conrad Vincent was something of a visionary and many of his ideas were literally years ahead of their time. That cantilever suspension, a hydraulic clutch, even a front-wheel-drive car, were all established through the Vincent decades before becoming common currency. Perhaps it was just as well that his inventive mind contained an entrepreneurial streak. If Vincent had not decided to set up on his own and join the British motorcycle industry, it is likely that his free-ranging ideas would have been quickly diluted, if not stifled altogether.

He certainly had an unconventional upbringing; his father was English but owned a ranch in Argentina, where Philip was born in 1908. In the manner of the time, he was sent away to England for his education, and it was at Harrow that he developed an interest in motorcycles that was to dominate the rest of his life. He outlined his cantilever rear suspension at the age of 17, went to Cambridge to study engineering, but soon decided that he needed to be in the trade as soon as possible. So he persuaded his father to put up the money to buy HRD.

HRD had been a short-lived success. Howard R. Davies (hence the name) was himself something of a character. Apprenticed at AJS, he rode in the TT, was a pilot during World War I, was shot down and was taken prisoner. There was more TT success after the war before Davies decided, in a Vincent-like manner, that contemporary machines simply weren't up to the job, to build his own bike around a JAP single. Unveiled at the 1924 Motorcycle Show at Olympia in London, the first HRD was admired for its quality and looks. Davies rode it at the TT the

Fast, expensive and long-lived, many Vincents are still in active use

following year, coming second in the Junior race and winning the Senior. Sadly, he was less successful as a businessman; the HRD's high price was enough to stifle sales, and the company went into liquidation.

It was bought by one Ernie Humphries, who seems to have done little with it, for in 1927 Philip Vincent came along with £400 and bought the name and its illustrious, albeit brief history.

Irving Arrives
The new Vincent-HRD company set up shop on the Great North Road in Stevenage, and went to work. Its first products used JAP engines (as had HRD), ohv singles of 350, 500 and 600cc (21, 30.5 and 37cu in). Of course, its unique point was Vincent's

rear suspension system, which used a pivoting triangular rear frame, with the spring units almost horizontal under the seat. They failed to meet with immediate success, one reason being that, amazing as it might seem now, rear suspension was viewed with suspicion. The company almost collapsed, but fortunately an enthusiastic customer named Bill Clarke persuaded his father to step in and save it and Captain Clarke became chairman. (Sadly, Vincent's own father had lost the ranch to an unreliable partner, so wasn't in a position to help.)

Help of a different kind arrived in 1931. Phil Irving's name has become as associated with the company as that of Vincent himself. An Australian engineer, Irving came to join Vincent-HRD by chance. Jack

Gill had ridden a Vincent and sidecar from England to Australia in 1929/30. At Melbourne, his passenger decided to quit, and Irving (presumably on a whim) took his place, returning to England with Gill and joining the company forthwith. Phil Irving was a wonderful production engineer, and much has been written concerning his place in the Vincent company: 'PCV' the engineering idealist, down-to-earth Irving who turned his visions into reality. What is clear is that both men contributed hugely to Vincent-HRD and the company and its motorcycles would not have been the same without either of them.

Over the next few years, the two Phils designed and produced a number of different bikes, still with JAP engines, which began to win acceptance through competition success, while Vincent continued to experiment with new ideas. One such was the balance beam braking system which used two drum brakes on each wheel controlled by a single cable via a balance beam. They also entered three JAP-powered bikes for the 1934 TT but, when all three broke down, thoughts turned to producing their own engine.

The Comet 499cc single was the result. It had a relatively short stroke for the time, with high-mounted camshaft (to allow shorter, stiffer pushrods) and a 6.8 or 7.3:1 compression ratio. Set in a frame with Vincent's rear suspension, it produced 26bhp at 5,600rpm in higher Comet tune and could push the bike to 145km/h (90mph), while a more highly tuned TT Replica broached 100mph. It was less well known than the V-twin, but the 500 single remained a part of the Vincent range almost to the end.

There is more than one story of how the Meteor single became a V-twin, the most attractive of which was that two drawings of the single were blown together by a breeze, noticed by Phil Irving, and the rest is history. Whatever the truth, Philip

Vincent was equally enthusiastic about the idea (one of his visions had been a gentleman's high-speed motorcycle, a kind of two-wheeled Bentley), and in just three months they had a bike ready for the 1936 Motorcycle Show. The Series A Rapide

produced 45bhp, which doesn't sound much now but was enough for a 174km/h (108mph) top speed and an effortless, loping cruise on the high gearing. Also enough, in any case, to make the 998cc (61cu in) twin the fastest production

motorcycle of its day. However, only 78 were sold before war broke out, simply because Vincent-HRD was still a very small company that could not afford to spend much on expanding production.

Oddly enough, it was the war that

OPPOSITE and ABOVE: Black Prince with and without modern add-ons

changed all that. Vincent switched from motorcycles to bomb fuses and other bits and pieces for the duration and it is difficult to imagine army despatch riders being issued with 100mph Rapides. It also had a contract to develop a two-stroke twin (already patented by PCV) for life-boats, and part of the deal was a well-equipped engine test house and more machine-shop capacity, all at the taxpayers' expense. So at the war's end, Vincent and Irving (who had left to join Velocette in 1936, but returned to assist with the boat project) were able to update the Rapide, and prepare to build it in respectable numbers.

Quality Costs

It was more of a full-scale redesign than a simple update. The engine became unit-constructed (15 years before the main British factories made the change), acquired alloy cylinder barrels and heads, and was now a stressed member of the new frame, which replaced the conventional tubular frame. That was another Vincent innovation: using the engine as a load-bearing part of the chassis is now the norm, but in 1945 it was a new idea. But far from being an impractical toy, the Series B Rapide bristled with convenience features: the seat was height-adjustable (how many machines offer that now?); the rear wheel could be removed in less than a minute; all controls were adjustable; an optional rear wheel for sidecar users could be reversed, with a sidecar-geared sprocket on the other side. None of this was cheap, of course, and the Series B cost twice as much as a big BSA or Triumph. But it was beautifully made, long-lived and well-mannered, not to mention faster than anything else on the road.

Faster perhaps, but there was plenty of potential inside the mildly tuned V-twin for still more performance, as the famous 'Gunga Din' was to prove. This was a 1947 Rapide rejected by the test department as below standard, but after attention from Irving and the Brown brothers, proved astonishingly fast. Records for tracks, hillclimbs and outright speed were broken by this one bike, which gave Vincent the idea for a more sporting Rapide. The Black Shadow of 1948 was the result, tuned to produce 55bhp and easily capable of 193km/h (120mph). More speed was to come: Rollie Free reached 238km/h (148mph) on a tuned Shadow at Bonneville salt flats, to take the world speed record for an unsupercharged bike. It wasn't quite enough for Rollie, who immediately stripped down to his bathing trunks and lay horizontally along the machine in an attempt to reach 150mph! He did it.

Meanwhile, the Vincent single had returned, first as the Meteor, then as the developed Comet and more sporting Grey Flash. Overshadowed by the twins, it was never a great success, though even this the most expensive single-cylinder bike in the world offered Vincent design and quality at a lower price than the Rapide. In 1949, the latter was updated into Series C form, notably with the addition of Girdraulic forks. It was a time when other manufacturers were switching to the new hydraulically-damped telescopic forks, but typically, Irving and Vincent knew they could do better. The Girdraulics used two strong blades of aircraft quality L64 alloy, with forged steel yokes and long enclosed springs. Far stronger and more rigid than conventional forks, but just as soft in action,

ABOVE: Egli–Vincent at Daytona

RIGHT: Vincent-HRD 500 Comet single

they kept the wheelbase constant and did not dive under braking. They were (inevitably) more costly than telescopics and needed to be properly maintained, but the Girdraulics were a typically advanced Vincent solution. (There are some similarities to BMW's Telelever system, introduced in the early 1990s.)

In 1949, with the Series C seen into production, Phil Irving decided to return to Australia and, according to some, development then entered a quiet phase until the Series D of 1955. By now, the Vincent twin was beginning to look a little elderly, despite its still-advanced features, though it was selling well and remained the fastest bike you could buy at any price. Philip Vincent was quite in favour of diversification, however, taking over the Firefly cyclemotor from Miller (a company which had long supplied Vincent's electrical equipment) and built 3,000 of them. There

was also an agreement with the importer of the NSU Quickly to sell this little German moped and assemble 98/125cc (6/8cu in) NSUs at Stevenage. Alas, the Quickly was so successful that the U.K. importer lost no time in taking the concession back.

The time was nearing for Vincent's swansong, the Series D. Although some long-standing complaints were addressed (notably through more reliable coil ignition, and a steering damper) the Series D's main feature couldn't be missed – it had all-enclosing bodywork. PCV had been keen on this idea for years, and had offered it on some pre-war machines, but with other British factories making tentative moves in this direction, he decided the time was right. A large black fibreglass fairing protected the rider, with side panels hiding most of the mechanics from view. The Black Knight (in Rapide tune) and Black Shadow (Shadow) certainly gave more

protection than the naked bikes, and were more economical at speed, though ultimately not quite as fast. Once again, Vincent proved himself far ahead of his time, for now most high-speed sports-tourers are similarly enclosed.

Sadly, it was not enough. Despite full order books in 1955, Philip Vincent decided to cease production altogether. Costs continued to spiral upwards, and the company was now losing money on every machine. Motorcycle sales were declining

at home, while vital U.S. exports were controlled by businessman Joe Berliner, who was said to drive a very hard bargain indeed. Vincent the company was taken over in 1959, while Philip was beset by illness and financial problems: he died in 1979. But his bikes lived on, and the efforts of the Vincent Owners Club to again manufacture spares has ensured that Vincent V-twins (the 'Snarling Beasts') will be roaring over our roads for yet a while.

VINCO *England 1903–05*
Used the 211cc (13cu in) Minerva favoured by many pioneers.

VINDEC *England 1902–29*
Produced a range, often of JAP-engined bikes of 172–490cc (10.5–30cu in), under its proprietors the Brown brothers.

VINDEC-SPECIAL *England 1903–14*
A rebadged Allright for the English market, built in Germany.

VIPER *England 1919–22*
A step-through frame and 293cc (18cu in) JAP sv.

VIRATELLE *France 1907–24*
Produced a variety of models with bought-in engines.

VIS *Germany 1923–25*
249cc (15cu in) single or 496cc (30cu in) fore-aft flat-twin two-strokes.

VITTORIA *Italy 1931–80*
Brand name used by Carnielli. Used Sachs, JAP, Küchen or Python power units, but mostly 98cc (6cu in) two-strokes after 1945.

VOLLBLUT *Germany 1925–27*
Utilized 248/348cc (15/21cu in) Blackburne ohv singles.

VORAN *Germany 1921–24*
A 143cc (9cu in) three-port two-stroke lightweight.

VOSKHOD *Former U.S.S.R. 1966–*
Brand name used on a 174cc (11cu in) two-stroke, which owes something to DKW and Jawa.

VOXAN *France 1999–*
In the 1990s, the European motorcycle industry, not to mention Harley-Davidson and its new home-grown rivals, seemed to be undergoing a true renaissance. Triumph had returned, BMW prospered, Ducati was reaching new heights, and a rapidly expanding Cagiva was restoring MV Agusta to life. Only France, of the once-major motorcycle producers, seemed to be the odd one out.

Jacques Gardette had other plans. A successful businessman, who happened to ride a Ducati 916, he was frustrated by the lack of a home-grown French industry and decided to follow John Bloor's example and set some up. From 1995, he began to attract finance from government agencies and Michelin, not to mention his own investment. Chassis designer Alain Chevallier was taken on to produce the first major new French motorcycle for 50 years, and in late 1998 it was revealed.

Its basis was a 72-degree one-litre V-twin with fuel injection, dohc and eight valves. While not as overtly sporting as the Italian opposition, the new bike was certainly up-to-the-minute, with a light (9kg/20lb) twin tubular frame that used the engine as a stressed member. One interesting point was that the head angle could easily be changed by swapping the chassis' headstock casting. Fuel was carried low down behind the V-twin with a dummy fuel tank actually housing the airbox. Rear suspension was by monoshock, mounted Buell-style underneath the engine, but working in compression rather than extension. In standard form, the new engine produced 108bhp at 9,000rpm and 80lb ft at 7,000rpm, though it was also destined for the half-faired Café Racer Voxan, which

ABOVE: The German-made VS lasted only a few years

BELOW: Voyager promised a new style of motorcycling

promised 120bhp. A more relaxed 1240cc (76cu in) version was planned for a cruiser and fully-faired tourer.

Alan Cathcart was one of the first journalists to ride the Voxan in October 1998, and was duly impressed. 'What Voxan has done,' he wrote in *Motorcycle Sport & Leisure*, 'is build the bike that Ducati has so far opted out of making. This is the first fuel-injected, eight-valve European V-twin sports roadster with superbike performance and a chassis package to suit.' And if in early 1999 the initial orders were anything to go by, the French buying public certainly agreed.

VOYAGER *Britain c.1990*
The Voyager was another attempt at producing a large feet-forward machine. Like the earlier Quasar, it used the Reliant four-cylinder car engine of 747cc (46cu in). With built-in luggage space and a car-type seat, it was a serious attempt at a practical all-round bike, and early road tests suggested that the Voyager had much promise. Sadly, the production versions were both heavier and slower, and only a few were sold.

VS *Germany 1922–24*
The VS was only made in limited numbers.

VULCAAN *The Netherlands 1911–27*
Built own singles and V-twins, possibly with help from the Zedel factory.

VULCAN *Czechoslovakia 1904–24*
Connected to Perun, it only manufactured spares after World War I.

VULCAN *England 1922–24*
Used mostly 248cc (15cu in) two-strokes, except for a 293cc (18cu in) sv JAP.

W

WACKWITZ *Germany 1920–22*
A 108cc (6.6cu in) clip-on.

WADDINGTON *England 1902–06*
Single-cylinder motorcycles with a variety of engines which included Minerva, MMC and other products.

WAG *England 1924–25*
A two-stroke V-twin of 496cc (30cu in) with limited production.

WAGNER *Czechoslovakia 1930–35*
Produced two- and four-strokes from 98–499cc (6–30cu in).

WAKEFIELD *England c.1902*
Utilized Minerva or MMC engines in cycle frames.

WALBA *Germany 1949–52*
Ilo-engined scooters of 98–173cc (6–11cu in).

WALLIS *England 1925–26*
Notable for its hub-centre-steering. Engines were JAP ohv singles.

WALMET *Germany 1924–26*
Used its own 246cc (15cu in) two-stroke or a Kühne ohv 346cc (21cu in) unit.

WALTER *Germany 1903–42*
Used Fafnir engines first, later Villiers two-strokes, and finally a 98cc (6cu in) Sachs.

WALTER *Czechoslovakia 1900–49*
Josef Walter built his own singles and V-twins, leaving the company to set up another (below), and building a 496cc (30cu in) sv single and some racing ohc singles. Taken over by CZ in 1949.

WALTER *Czechoslovakia 1923–26*
A 746cc (45.5cu in) transverse V-twin, mainly for the Czech Army.

WANDERER *Germany 1902–29*
Well-respected maker of singles (327/387cc/20/24cu in) and V-twins (408/616cc/25/38cu in) before World War I, adding a 184cc (11cu in) ohv after 1918, plus unit-construction V-twins to 749cc/46cu inches (some eight-valved). A new 498cc (30cu in) unit-construction ohv single was on the drawing board in 1927, but was sold to Jawa before it reached production.

WARD *England 1915–16*
298cc (18cu in) two-strokes.

WARDILL *England 1924–26*
An unusual 346cc (21cu in) two-stroke single, with separate charging cylinder.

WARRIOR *England 1921–23*
Utilized a 247cc (15cu in) Villiers engine.

WATNEY *England 1922–23*
Used Villiers, JAP or Blackburne engines to 345cc (21cu in).

WAVERLEY *England 1921–23*
Used 269cc (16cu in) Peco two-strokes or 346/496cc (21/30cu in) Blackburne sv power units.

WD *England 1911–13*
An ioe 496cc (30cu in) single.

WEARWELL *England 1901–c.1906*
2.5/3.25hp engines from the Stevens brothers (pre-AJS days). Also built Wolfruna and Wolf machines and sold frames to others.

WEATHERELL *England 1922–23*
Used ohv Blackburne engines only, from 248–676cc (15–41cu in).

WEAVER *England 1922–25*
Began with a 142cc (9cu in) ohv single and was soon offering two-strokes as well.

WEBER-MAG *Germany 1926–27*
Used MAG engines of up to 746cc (45.5cu in).

WEBER & REICHMANN
Czechoslovakia 1923–26
Licence-built DKW frames with two-stroke engines direct from DKW.

WECOOB *Germany 1925–30*
Had a small production but large range, with power from the 142cc (9cu in) Rinne to 996cc (61cu in) JAP.

WEE McGREGOR *England 1922–25*
Not Scottish, but a 170cc (10cu in) two-stroke made in Coventry.

WEGRO *Germany 1922–23*
A 452cc (28cu in) two-stroke twin with long wheelbase.

WELA *Germany 1925–27*
Used a 348cc (21cu in) Kühne ohv engine.

WELLER *England 1902–05*
Used its own 1.75/2.25hp power units.

WELS *Germany 1925–26*
Used 348cc (21cu in) Kühne and 490cc (30cu in) JAP engines.

WELT-RAD *Germany 1901–07*
A 3.5hp single and 6hp V-twin.

WERNER *Germany 1897–1908*
The Werner brothers were first to place the engine at the base of the frame, a huge step forward away from the motorized bicycle and towards the true motorcycle. Built both singles and vertical twins, and sold their engines to other manufacturers.

WERNER-MAG *Austria 1928–30*
Used MAG engines in a 498cc (30cu in) single and V-twins up to 996cc (61cu in).

WERNO *Germany 1925–30*
Choice of a 143cc (9cu in) two-stroke or 154cc (9.4cu in) four-stroke.

WESPE *Austria 1937–38*
A Villiers-engined 122cc (7.4cu in) lightweight.

WESTFALIA *Germany 1901–06*
Mostly used De Dion and Fafnir engines.

WESTFIELD *England c.1903*
2.75hp MMC power units.

WESTOVIAN *England 1914–16*
Used bought-in engines (including JAPs and Villiers) from 197–498cc (12–30cu in).

WFM *Poland 1947–*
123–173cc (7.5–11cu in) two-strokes.

W&G *England 1927–28*
A two-stroke flat twin of 490cc (30cu in).

WHEATCROFT *England 1924*
Offered a two-stroke, the 318cc (19cu in)
Dalm, and the four-stroke 546cc (33cu in)
Blackburne sv.

WHIPPET *England 1903–c.1906*
Used 1.75–3hp engines and Aster and FN
units among others.

WHIPPET *England 1920–59*
A 180cc (11cu in) ohv single scooter with
16-inch wheels.

WHIPPET *England 1957–59*
Part scooter, part moped, with 49–64cc
(3–4cu in) power.

WHIRLWIND *England 1901–03*
A 1.5hp clip-on and 2/2.5hp machines.

WHITE & POPPE *England 1902–22*
Sold its engines to both car and motorcycle
manufacturers, as well as producing
complete machines which included 498cc
(30cu in) vertical twins, and 347cc
(21cu in) two-strokes.

WHITLEY *England 1902–c.1906*
Produced 2.75/3.5hp singles and sold its
engines to others.

WHITWOOD *England 1934–36*
A motorcycle with a car-like body like the
earlier German-made Mauser, with
248–490cc (15–30cu in) JAP engines.

ABOVE: A 1950 199cc (12cu in) Whizzer

WHIZZER *U.S.A. 1947–54*
A 199cc (12cu in) sv single scooter.

WIGA *Germany 1928–32*
Utilized 198–498cc (12–30cu in) JAP and
ohc Küchen power units.

WIGAN-BARLOW *England 1921*
Used 293cc (18cu in) sv JAP and 346
(21cu in) Barr & Stroud sleeve-valved
singles.

WIKRO *Germany 1924–26*
Used Precision and Blackburne engines.

WILBEE *England 1902–c.1906*
Used 2hp Minerva engines.

WILHELMINA *The Netherlands
1903–15*
A 2.5hp Precision single.

ABOVE: A 1914 Williamson

WILIER *Italy 1962–c.1970*
Made 49cc (3cu in) mopeds and
lightweights.

WILKIN *England 1919–23*
Used 346/499cc (21/30cu in) sv
Blackburne engines in sprung frames.

WILKINSON-ANTOINE *England
1903–06*
Bought-in Belgian Antoine singles of 2.25
and 2.75hp.

**WILKINSON-TAC (WILKINSON
TMC)** *England 1909–16*
The same Wilkinson that still makes
razor-blades, it then offered an air-cooled
four of 676cc/41cu inches (later
844cc/51.5cu in) with rear suspension
and a bucket seat.

BELOW: Four-cylinder Wilkinson

WILLIAMS *U.S.A. 1912–20*
Built its single-cylinder engine into the rear
wheel.

WILLIAMSON *England 1912–20*
Early bikes used an air/water-cooled 996cc
(61cu in) flat twin, later a 770cc (47cu in)
JAP V-twin.

WILLOW *England 1920*
A 269cc (16cu in) Villiers-powered scooter.

WIMMER *Germany 1921–39*
Made a 134cc (8cu in) clip-on, and a variety of lightweight and mid-sized bikes up to 497cc (30cu in), both water- and air-cooled

WIN *England 1908–14*
Used 499 and 599cc (30 and 37cu in) Precision singles.

WINCO *England 1920–22*
Used a 261cc (16cu in) Orbit two-stroke.

WINDHOFF *Germany 1924–33*
An interesting range of bikes, including water-cooled two-strokes of 122/173cc (7.4/11cu in). Also an oil-cooled ohc 746cc (45.5cu in) four which was used as a stressed member and was shaft-driven as well. Produced a prototype 996cc (61cu in) flat twin later. Last bikes were quite conventional Villiers-powered lightweights.

WITTEKIND *Germany 1952–54*
Produced mopeds with 40cc (2.4cu in) Komet engines.

WITTLER Germany *1924–53*
Used own 249cc (15cu in) two-stroke before the war, and resumed in 1949 with Sachs or Zündapp-powered mopeds.

WIZARD *Wales 1920–22*
A 269cc (16cu in) Liberty two-stroke.

WK *Germany 1920–22*
A 249cc (15cu in) sv for bicycles, for building into the wheel.

WKB *Austria 1923–24*
A 183cc (11cu in) three-port two-stroke.

WMB *Germany 1924–26*
Built own 1.8hp sv engine.

WOLF *England 1901–39*
All engines were bought in from Moto-Rêve in early years, with Villiers, Blackburnes and JAPs later on, to 678cc (41cu in).

WOOLER *England 1911–55*
All of John Wooler's designs were unusual, notably the 344cc (21cu in) double-ended piston two-stroke (one end acted as compressor) and the 346/496cc (21/30cu in) flat twins with side-mounted (but ohv) valves. After 1945, a small number of shaft-driven flat fours were sold.

The unusual two-stroke Wooler was always unique

WOTAN *Germany 1923–25*
A 170cc (10.4cu in) three-port two-stroke.

WSE *Germany 1924–25*
Built own 249cc (15cu in) sv.

WSK *Poland 1946–*
123–240cc (7.5–14.6cu in) two-strokes, the 125 being the longest-lived derivative of DKW's RT125.

WSM *Germany 1919–23*
Built a few complete bikes, and sold 496cc (30 cu in) flat twins to Victoria.

WUCO *Germany 1925*
Offered own 174cc (11cu in) sv, and bigger JAPs up to 490cc (30cu in).

WURRING *Germany 1921–59*
Also sold as the AWD and used a large variety of bought-in engines of 142–596cc (9–36cu in).

WÜRTTEMBERGIA *Germany 1925–33*
Used only Blackburne engines from 198–596cc (12–36cu in).

W&W *Austria 1925–27*
Mostly used MAG 498cc (30cu in) singles, but V-twins were made to order.

X

XL *England 1921–23*
Used JAP or Blackburne sv singles to 538cc (33cu in).

XL-ALL *England 1902–c.1906*
Built own small 90-degree V-twins of 2 and 4hp.

Y

YALE *U.S.A. 1902–1915*
A big, typically American V-twin of 950cc (58cu in), with early use of chain-drive.

YAMAGUCHI *Japan 1941–64*
Produced mostly 49cc (3cu in) mopeds, plus a 123cc (7.5cu in) two-stroke twin.

YAMAHA *Japan 1953–*
Torakusu Yamaha, whose name graces the sides of millions of motorcycles did not, as far as we know, ride one himself. In fact, as he died in 1916, he may never have even seen a motorcycle, for which an explanation is required.

Yamaha was born in Nagasaki in 1851 and was first apprenticed to a clock maker,

war production of musical instruments was subsumed by military work.

In 1948, sufficient normality was restored to allow for the manufacture of instruments to begin once more, though only two years later Kawakami passed the presidency to his son, Genichi. One of his first acts as president was to utilize the wartime machinery which was lying idle, and one of the best uses was to build a small motorcycle for Japan's rapidly growing home market. With no experience of bikes, the company sensibly based its design on an existing one, namely the DKW RT125, which was the same DKW copied by BSA for the Bantam and Harley-Davidson for the Hummer, though there were others. Being well-established with capital behind it, Nippon Gakki could afford to take its time perfecting the new

ABOVE: Sales brochure for Yamaha V50, very similar to the Honda Cub

BELOW: The DS two-stroke twin survived until 1973

then to a manufacturer of medical equipment. He moved to Hamamatsu in 1883, then working as a self-employed engineer, where he was asked to repair the organ at the local primary school. Yamaha evidently found this interesting as he decided to go into the musical instrument business himself. Nippon Gakki, it was called, and it thrived and was soon a major force in the market, which is why the Yamaha logo to this day consists of three tuning forks. But after Yamaha's death, the company acquired an apparently dictatorial head named Chiymanu Amano, who was present during a number of strikes, not to mention the Kano earthquake of 1923. Order was restored by Kaichi Kawakami, who took over as president in 1926. His team-building approach paid dividends and Nippon Gakki recovered, though during the

Yamaha always sold as many commuters as sportsbikes

bike while building a brand new factory for it at Hamamatsu. And the name of the new motorcycle division? In honour of the company's founder, it would be 'Yamaha'.

That first machine, the 125cc YA1, did much for Yamaha's image by winning national races and, by the end of 1955, the company was building 200 a month. A larger 175cc (11cu in) version, still DKW-based, went on sale for 1956 and the YA series continued until the early 1970s. A 250 was the next step, and the obvious thing was to base it on an existing bike. The DKW 250 was rejected as being a single, and an Adler MB250 twin was bought instead. But once it was there, the design head considered their own 250 could do better. This was agreed, and Yamaha's YD1 was the result, sharing nothing with the Adler apart from basic layout and dimensions. A successful road

bike with a period pressed steel frame, it gave 17bhp.

Encouraged by its early race successes, the company built a works racing version of the YD1, with a lighter, stronger tubular frame and even a short-stroke version of the motor. It was rewarded with a 1-2-3 in the Asama races in 1957, plus first and second in the 125cc race. Rival Honda had been conclusively beaten, and orders for the YD1 began to flow in. It is illuminating that, so early on, Yamaha had discovered the sales advantage that competition success could bring. Maybe this was why racing of all kinds has been so central to the company's activities ever since. Thus it was the first Japanese company to race in America, and plunged into European Grand Prix racing in 1961, scoring 7th in both 125 and 250 French GPs.

Racing Pays Off

So not long after its very first motorcycle (based on a pre-war DKW) went on sale, Yamaha was competitive in international racing. It had a slight headstart by taking over the Showa marque in 1959, whose 125cc racer was very fast and taught Yamaha much about disc valves. Unlike Honda, Yamaha at the time was still wedded to the two-stroke engine, whether for its racers or for a simple commuter like the 80cc (5cu in) YG1, which was launched in the early sixties, but was still on sale as the YB100 30 years later. Although those early Japanese machines might look a little basic nowadays, they were actually quite advanced, the YB100 having automatic oiling (no tiresome pre-mix) and a disc valve (the racing influence), plus an impressive 10bhp. Practical and reliable as well as nippy, it is

no wonder they sold so well.

A twin-cylinder 100, the YL1, appeared in 1966, though this one only lasted five years. It could manage 113km/h (70mph) in standard guise (not far behind some European 250s) and true to form, Yamaha offered a race kit which nearly doubled the power. The YDS series were 250 twins, starting with the YDS1 in 1959, updated into the YDS2 (1962) and YDS3 (1964). All were 246cc (15cu in) piston-ported twins, with 28bhp at 8,000rpm. There was also a 305cc (19cu in) YM1. They eventually developed into the DS7, which itself was the immediate precursor of the long-running RD-series. All these were road bikes, but just as important to Yamaha were the TD-series of off-the-shelf racers, starting with the 250cc (15cu in) TD1 in 1962, plus the 350cc (21cu in) TR-series, which was to become the liquid-cooled TZ from 1969. That Yamaha was able to sell these racers was down to its own success. Remember the European debut in 1961? Yamaha couldn't afford to race in Europe in 1962, but the year after saw a determined assault with the 250cc RD56, now with 45bhp at 11,000rpm. Yamaha was rewarded with its first GP win on the Spa circuit in Belgium, plus second places in Holland and the Isle of Man. The following year, Phil Read won the 250cc World Championship for Yamaha, and again in 1965. They couldn't match the Hailwood/Honda combination in 1966/67, but won both 125 and 250 titles in 1968, though both Honda and Suzuki had pulled out at the end of the previous season.

That same year, Yamaha announced something new. It was now exporting successfully to the United States where, by

BELOW: The Yamaha 350 autolube, with late sixties performance

ABOVE: 1976 Trail 50

the late sixties, the market for dual-purpose trail bikes, as happy off the road as on it, was growing rapidly. Yamaha's importer persuaded the factory that what was needed was something close to the off-road ability of a Greeves or Bultaco, but with more civilized on-road manners. The DT1 was the result, and it was truly a new type of bike. The 175cc (11cu in) two-stroke single was relatively comfortable and easy to ride; it was well silenced, had good lights, and cruised happily at 97km/h (60mph), yet it could also take to the dirt if you so wished. (DT stood for 'Dirt Trail'.) It was a hit, and Yamaha's competitors soon came out with trail bikes of their own. So successful was the DT that a whole range of bikes grew up around it, from a DT50 to the relatively short-lived DT400. It was said that, like luxury 4x4 vehicles, some of these trail bikes never got their tyres muddy – it was the suggestion of trailing that riders wanted.

Although the DT opened up a new market, it wasn't that difficult for Yamaha to produce, being a two-stroke. The XS1, unveiled the following year, couldn't have been more different. It was the largest bike Yamaha had ever built, and it was a four-stroke. The basic idea was a sound one: take the highly popular (but increasingly outmoded) British vertical-twin concept and update it to take up where the Bonneville had left off. The XS certainly looked good on paper, being a 653cc (40cu in) twin with overhead cam, five-speed gearbox and electric start, plus Japanese reliability. It wasn't an instant success, for at the time Japanese manufacturers had yet to master the art of motorcycle roadholding and handling, especially with the larger

bikes. However, Yamaha persevered, and the revamped, renamed XS650 was developed into quite a decent bike, acquiring a following of its own. The torquey engine was to prove adept at sidecar motocross and American flat-track racing. A measure of its eventual success is that Yamaha went on making it until the early 1980s.

However, one development didn't get that far. The TX750 was a bored out version of the 650, though as Triumph was finding out at the same time (this was 1972), 750cc (46cu in) was really too much for an unbalanced vertical twin. Yamaha accepted this, and designed a balancer system (two counter-rotating weights in the rear of the crankcase) to counteract the vibration. It worked, and the 750 was certainly smoother than the 650. Unfortunately, the crankshaft-driven balancer sapped so much power that the TX was actually slower than the smaller bike, struggling to even reach 161km/h (100mph). It was ignominiously dropped, just a few months after launch.

Two-Stroke Days

Meanwhile, Yamaha was having a happier time with what it knew best – small two-strokes. The company had noted the huge success of Honda's Cub and like Suzuki came up with something very similar to meet it though, being a Yamaha, it was a two-stroke. It came in V50 and V80 forms, both having reed-valves. The smaller had a two-speed automatic gearbox (though with manual selection) and the 79cc (4.8cu in) V80 was a three-speeder. Naturally, the two-stroke oil was mixed automatically, while drive was by enclosed chain. These two were later replaced by the four-stroke T50 and T80, both of which boasted the sophistication of shaft-drive. The earlier step-thrus offered no real advantage over the Honda, though that wasn't really the point – they gave Yamaha something to sell in this fiercely competitive market.

A more obvious class leader was the FS1 sports moped, which first appeared in 1972 and is actually still being made, though in restricted, sanitized form only. With its disc-valved engine and motorcycle looks, the FS1E was the bike for 16-year-olds to be seen on in 1970s Britain. There were daring tales of 52, even 53mph on the right downhill stretch, when the author's Puch could barely manage 61km/h (38mph) on a good day! However, laws changed and these sports mopeds were restricted back to a maximum of 30mph. But it is still on sale, 20 years later, in drum-braked (FS1) or disc-braked (FS1DX) forms.

If our sports moped rider survived the FS1E, he (and they usually were, though not exclusively male) would often graduate to a DT175. Of all Yamaha's DT trail bike series, the 175 was possibly the best compromise. It had enough performance to be exciting, yet was light enough to take off-road easily, and much cheaper on fuel and insurance than the 250 and 400. No wonder it enjoyed a production run of 12 years (1973–1985).

Among certain generations of riders, the letters 'FS1E' and 'DT' have a certain resonance, but none can compete with the magical 'RD' (apart perhaps from its successor, the 'LC'). RD in this case stood for 'Race Developed' which in Yamaha's case had more than an element of truth in

Yamaha Tenere, a 660cc (40cu in) five-valve single, was inspired by Paris–Dakar racers

it, rooted as the company was in racing air-cooled two-stroke twins. The RD-series replaced the long-running YDS in 1973, and its main advance was the use of reed-valve induction in place of conventional piston ports. Reed valves were not a new concept, and the basic idea is simple. Instead of relying on the passing piston to open and close off each port, the reed is a flap valve, sucked open by the vacuum under a rising piston, and closing as the piston descends. A key advantage is that

ports are less compromised in shape and the power band is wider. But Yamaha's version used an innovation of its own, an extra transfer port above the inlet port, which drew in an extra helping of charge after the main one and improved scavenging as well. Perfect scavenging (the evacuation of all exhaust gases from the cylinder to allow a full fresh charge to come in) is the object of every two-stroke. In practical terms, this meant that the new RD250's power band now started at

4,000rpm instead of the previous 6,000rpm, with obvious benefits in rideability and fuel consumption.

Yamaha demonstrated its faith in the new system (which rejoiced in the marketing-friendly term of 'Torque Induction') by launching a whole range of RDs within a couple of months of one another. There was an RD125 (124cc/8cu in), RD200 (196cc/12cu in), RD250 (247cc/15cu in) and RD350 (347cc/21cu in). The two larger bikes had a six-speed

Competition success has been important to Yamaha. This is a 250cc (15cu in) enduro bike

ABOVE: 1980s XJ650   *BELOW: 750 Super Tenere*   *ABOVE: A straightforward XJ550*

gearbox which, according to author Mick Walker, was merely a convenient means of homologating the TZ racer's gearbox. Those early RDs looked very similar to the older YDS, but all had a comprehensive restyle in 1975, with squared-off tank and seat and block-style graphics that became the RD trademark. At the same time, the RD125 and 200 acquired front disc brakes. A year later, the RD350 became the RD400, due to an 8mm longer stroke, with 40bhp and a stronger bottom-end to suit. After that, there were just minor changes, though electronic ignition was a worthwhile advance in 1978. However, the RD two-strokes, for all their power, were simply unable to meet imminent U.S. emissions limits, and the whole range was dropped in 1980.

XS & LC

It is odd that while Yamaha was producing such class-leading and popular two-strokes, its four-strokes should still be relatively lacklustre. At first glance, the XS500 twin announced in 1975 looked promising: twin overhead camshafts, four valves per cylinder, and a balancer shaft to dampen the vibration. The all-new engine produced a claimed 48bhp at 8,500rpm for a top speed of 175km/h (109mph). Unfortunately, the 500 was a weighty old thing at over 200kg (441lb) with disappointing acceleration and no real get up and go. The lighter, simpler XS twins sold rather better. First was the XS360 of 1976, with single overhead cam and 180-degree crankshaft. An XS250 followed, while the 360 was later bored out to 399cc/24cu inches, all three bikes

The TZ 750 two-stroke did well in circuit racing, but is shown here adapted for the American dirt track

The shaft-drive, three-cylinder XS750

ABOVE and OPPOSITE: XS850 was an update of the XS750

sharing the same 52.4mm stroke. The 400 actually lasted up to 1983, by which time it had a new backbone frame, twin overhead-cam cylinder head and monoshock rear suspension. It is still not remembered with quite the same affection as the RD.

There was a lot more anticipation when the XT500 trail bike was launched in 1977. Although rather heavy for serious off-road use, it echoed the DT in opening up a new market for trail bikes, in this case for big four-stroke singles which, until then, Japanese manufacturers had ignored. The 499cc (30cu in) single overhead-cam engine looked simple in the extreme with just two valves, one carburettor and no electric start. Indeed, some thought this was the long-awaited return of the simple,

torquey big single. But it put out confusing messages, with the ground clearance, suspension travel and seat height of a proper off-roader, together with that 138kg (304lb) mass.

Perhaps the SR500, a pure road bike, was a more honest use of the 499cc single. The engine was basically similar, but had larger valves and carburettor, and various parts strengthened to cope with high-speed cruising. There were also decent 12-volt electrics (the XT was 6-volt) and a disc front brake. Some were sold, but the SR wasn't really a modern BSA Gold Star.

But in the same year that the XT appeared, Yamaha also came up with its first truly successful four-stroke. The XS750 was its belated Superbike

competitor, and it was right first time. The 747cc (46cu in) dohc triple wasn't an out-and-out sportster; it was too heavy for that, and in any case the shaft-drive indicated that this was a bike with touring pretensions. Nor was it quite as fast, at 177km/h (110mph) as some other 750s, but it was smooth and comfortable. Performance was improved by an increase in capacity to 826cc (50cu in) in 1980, which took power up to 79bhp at 8,500rpm and top speed to 201km/h (125mph). And despite the weight it handled reasonably well, due to fully adjustable suspension at both ends. It was superseded by the four-cylinder XJ900 in 1983.

Despite its determination to break into the big four-stroke market, Yamaha's two-

strokes were still doing well on the track, especially the twin-cylinder production racers. It won the 250cc World Championship four times in the 1970s (1970–73) and the 350 class in the following three years, plus two 125cc titles. The 500 class came Yamaha's way in 1973, then (thanks to Kenny Roberts) from 1978–'80 as well. It was also developing a presence in off-road sport, winning motocross GPs by the middle of the decade.

Meanwhile, although the air-cooled RD had been killed off by U.S. regulations, the bike had been so successful in Europe that Yamaha decided to launch a replacement aimed specifically at the Europeans. Still a two-stroke twin, the big news was that it was liquid-cooled, which gave a more even-

POWERFUL AND SMOOTH, THE GRAND TOURER WITH THE SPORTING EDGE

The best in engineering is said to be a compromise. Perhaps so. But the only compromise Yamaha are prepared to make in our pursuit of perfection is the compromise between sheer inspiration and ceaseless development. That compromise, and no other, has produced the XS850.

The inspiration that produced the XS750 and led to its undisputed reign as the world's finest tourer lies at the heart of the new 850. The double-overhead-camshaft three-cylinder engine was perfect for its purpose. Powerful and smooth, it gave the grand tourer a sporting edge and a character that won it instant favour the world over. Now, we have given the 850 just a little more power, a little more torque, and perhaps still greater character.

The XS850 retains the features that gave the 750 its reputation — the shaft drive, the ultra-comfortable seat, and the Teflon-lined heavy-duty forks, while incorporating vital improvements. The 850 features new, upswept exhausts for extra ground clearance, a larger tank for still longer distances between fuel stops, and new 200mm halogen headlight. It also carries an oil cooler for enhanced reliability and still longer engine life.

The XS850 is the result of the only kind of compromise that Yamaha recognise: the compromise that seeks nothing short of perfection.

(Frame & suspension) The 850 employs the same superbly balanced double-loop cradle frame that gave the 750 its legendary handling. The Teflon-lined long-travel forks and the adjustable rear suspension ensure a balance of handling and comfort under all conditions, whatever the load. The 850 features a redesigned seat and newly styled exhausts to provide extra ground clearance.

To further extend the safety margin of the XS850, a more powerful 200mm halogen headlight has been fitted. Indicators are of Yamaha's self-cancelling design. Wheels are cast alloy in black and silver trim. There are two disc brakes on the front wheel, with rear-mounted calipers; the rear brake is a single disc.

(Engine & gearbox) The 826cm³ three-cylinder engine is perfectly suited to the role of sports touring. Developing 79hp at 8500rpm the three develops its maximum torque of 7.1kg-m at 7500, thus providing a forceful but usable spread of power. The overhead-camshaft unit is designed not only for supreme dependability, but to be delightfully smooth throughout its rev range. Long-distance rider fatigue is drastically cut.

A strong five-speed gearbox and a heavy-duty multiplate clutch are connected to the rear wheel by Yamaha's famous shaft-drive system. Completely free of drive-train snatch and torque reaction, the shaft is the most efficient and least demanding transmission system that can be fitted to a tourer. Maintenance is minimal and reliability is total.

BELOW: The V-twin XV1000, shown here in 'Midnight Special' guise

BELOW: A TZ750 racer

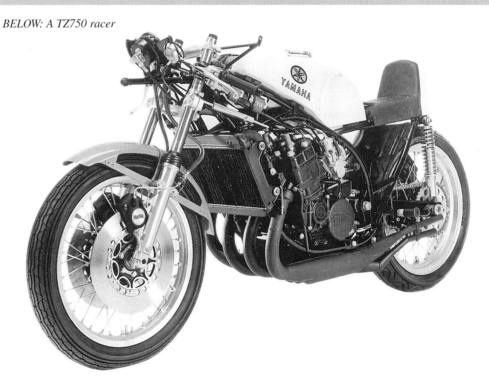

running temperature (both over time and over different parts of the engine) and less noise. Although it looked completely different to the old RD, with the squared-off shape giving way to a pleasing rounded form, the LC owed much to its predecessor. Reed-valve induction was still there, and the six-speed gearbox was familiar as well, but there was a new monoshock rear suspension (derived from the YZ motocrossers) and anti-vibration rubber mounting for the engine. Predictably, the LC (known as 'Elsie' to U.K. enthusiasts) became the bike to have in Production Racing, winning 250 and 500 classes in its first TT. The only big development of the bike was the Yamaha Power Valve System (YPVS) which was unveiled in 1982. Its impressive 59bhp at 9,000rpm was made

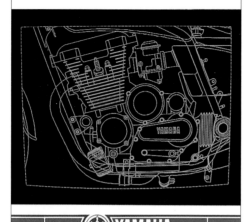

INNOVATIONS 1981 YAMAHA

YAMAHA

Yamaha's first bike (TOP RIGHT) was worlds apart from the bulky XS1100 (BELOW)

YAMAHA – ALWAYS LEADERS IN MOTORCYCLE DEVELOPMENT

It was in 1955, over a quarter of a century ago, that the first Yamaha motorcycle made its public debut.

That machine was a simple, single-cylinder 125cc two-stroke but, ever since that time, Yamaha has been in the forefront of motorcycling development.

Waterproof brakes, rotary valves, automatic oiling for two-strokes, reed valves, direct chrome plating of alloy cylinder bores, multiple transfer ports, omniphase crankshaft balancing, air-damped forks and monoshock suspension, eight-valve cylinder heads for four-stroke twins,

curved-spoke cast wheels .... Yamaha were responsible for the introduction of all these important technical advances to mass production motorcycling.

Now the innovations continue into the nineteen-eighties with six important developments this year in the fields of fuel consumption, suspension, transmission and general engine efficiency.

ABOVE: RD350 YPVS

possible by a variable exhaust port, whose size and position changed automatically according to engine revs.

YPVS was also fitted to the ultimate RD, the 499cc (30cu in) V4 of 1984. The RD500LC was built to capitalize on Grand Prix success, but owed more to the LC than Kenny Roberts' racer. The cleverly-designed motor used two crankshafts and four carburettors, while the four YPVS valves were mechanically linked, operated by a single servo motor. Not for the faint-hearted, this ultimate road-going two-stroke could run up 217km/h (135mph) on its 80bhp. At the other end of the scale there were also liquid-cooled RD80s and RD125LCs, plus an air-cooled RD50 (Yamaha seemed determined to make the most of that 'Race Developed' prefix!)

At this time there were less exciting

tiddlers from Hamamatsu as well. The SR500 had been followed by an SR250 and 125, though these were in a different mould being mild-mannered commuters with custom styling. And all this time Yamaha was selling a full range of tiddlers, examples being the Passola 50 and scooter-style 79cc (4.8cu in) Beluga.

It took Yamaha some time to follow the four-cylinder four-stroke route along which its Japanese rivals had already ventured. After vertical twins and triples, its next attempt at an alternative big four-stroke was the TR1. Launched in late 1980, this was a 981cc (60cu in) roadster in European style. To appeal to its chosen market, the TR1 was relatively simple: the 75-degree V-twin had single overhead cams and two valves per cylinder; there was an enclosed chain-drive, vertically-split crankcases and five-speed gearbox. The only newer elements were electronic advance for the ignition timing and monoshock rear suspension, which Yamaha had now been using for seven years. Alongside the TR1 was the basically similar but smaller-engined 740cc (45cu in) Virago, with shaft-drive and custom styling. Both used steel backbone frames.

If the TR1/Virago showed a traditionalist approach to the V-twin, the XZ550 announced a couple of years later couldn't have been more different, proving that Yamaha was nothing if not eclectic. This 70-degree 552cc (34cu in) V-twin was liquid-cooled, with dohc four-valve cylinder-heads, each with twin exhaust ports. The engine had a balance shaft and was unusually hung from the downtubes of the cradle-type frame. There was shaft-drive, trailing-axle front forks and

BELOW: Special fairing option for XS1100

Frame/Suspension
The strong, duplex cradle frame has been developed out of Yamaha's racing technology to withstand the stress at any speed of one of the world's most powerful motorcycle engines. Front forks are adjustable, large-diameter, long-travel, Teflon-coated units to absorb shock and to accommodate heavy braking. Rear suspension units are equipped for pre-load spring adjustment depending upon the road and weight conditions.

Tank/Styling
The elegantly purposeful looks of the XS1100 have won admirers throughout the world. From the strong, smooth lines of its 24-litre tank to its square-cut headlight and its gently upswept exhausts, the 1100 looks every inch the masterpiece of engineering it undoubtedly is.

Wheels/Brakes
Strong, flex-free cast-alloy wheels (19-inch front; 17-inch rear) carry V-rated tyres to get the power of the XS on to the road and keep it there in perfect safety. Brakes are two 298mm discs at the front and a disc of the same size at the rear.

Fairing
Recognising the rider's need to enjoy the potential of his motorcycle to the full without the constant battering of a high-speed airstream, Yamaha commissioned the design of an aerodynamic fairing. Available through Yamaha dealers, the fairing adds nothing to the total area of the bike/rider unit yet cuts drag by 15 percent and produces a remarkable down-force of 32 percent on the front wheel. The rider is fully protected and the handling of the machine, particularly at high speeds, is improved. Designed specifically to avoid altering the basic specification of the motor-cycle (for ease of fitting), the fairing employs the principle of a separate fairing to rotate with the handlebars. The screen can thus reach back to the rider, improving streamlining and avoiding the necessity for extra width. The fairing, which is the first of its kind in the world, has proved in independent tests to be superior in most respects to bulkier, more conventional streamlining.

The Virage 1100 was a popular factory custom

SRX600, a good-looking sporting single

unpleasant squared-off styling. In fact, the XZ550 resembled one of those concept bikes where every idea the R&D boys can come up with is thrown together on one machine in order to gauge reaction. In this case, all the gizmos added up to less than their sum, and performance was disappointing and problematic. Buyers could not be tempted, and the XZ was soon dropped.

Fours & Fives

But simultaneously with the XZ550, Yamaha was also selling a range of perfectly straightforward dohc fours. The XJ series began with a 550 before growing into the shaft-driven 650 and 750. None

made a huge impact apart from the XJ650 Turbo, which along with Honda's CX Turbo marked a brief flirtation with turbos as an alternative to big engines, neither being successful. What did succeed was the bigger XJ900, which was unveiled in 1983. It was a strong, torquey, fairly simple touring machine, with an 853cc (52cu in) dohc air-cooled four-cylinder engine and shaft-drive. The capacity was soon increased to 891cc (now with 91bhp) and the FJ900 was quite a success, still selling 16 years on. In much the same mould was the FJ1100 of 1984, still an air-cooled shaft-driven four, but with far more power, monoshock rear suspenson and an alloy frame. It could break the 241km/h

(150mph) barrier and dawdle through town at minimal revs, winning the big FJ many friends. It also had a capacity increase in 1986 to 1188cc (72.5cu in), as the FJ1200. There were more minor changes in 1988, but perhaps more significant was the ABS option launched in 1991. Like the XJ900, the FJ is still in production.

Maybe this success with the bigger fours gave Yamaha more confidence with the smaller ones. The Diversion 600 of 1991 certainly suggested this. There was nothing very radical about it, but it was a very good seller where the old XJ600 was not. Its 600cc (37cu in) four was a much simplified version of the Genesis concept (see below), still with a slant-forward

block, but with air-cooling and just two valves per cylinder. Despite, or perhaps because of the modest specification, the Diversion proved to be an excellent all-rounder, which is what many people still want from a bike. Available in naked and half-faired forms, it was good value and a deserved success. The 600cc class has moved on so fast in the nineties that the Diversion is now very much the budget option, the 95bhp Fazer 600 from 1998 being more contemporary, but it goes on selling nonetheless.

The V-Max, on the other hand, could never be described as a sensible all-rounder. Launched in 1985, it was an unashamed performance muscle machine, with sheer acceleration and speed (in a straight line) its single-purpose goal. It looked like nothing else, with the surprisingly compact liquid-cooled 1198cc (73cu in) V4 filling the frame completely. It was based on the V4 of the Gold Wing-style XVZ12, but with larger carburettors and valves, not to mention higher compression, stronger valve-springs and toughened bottom-end. It is hardly surprising that the V-Max became something of a cult bike.

Yamaha hadn't forgotten the trail bike market that it had pioneered, though it was now applying four-stroke technology. The XT500 wasn't perfect, but it persevered with the four-valve, twin-carburettor 558cc (34cu in) XT550 (and a smaller XT400),

which in turn was superseded by the XT600 and XT600Z Tenere. The latter came about due to the popularity of desert rallies such as the Paris–Dakar, where huge fuel tanks and long, tall suspension was part of the required look. An electric-start version followed in 1990, all part of the thorough updating of the XT concept which kept it selling. The road-going single wasn't neglected either, with the SR500 transformed into the SRX600, using the same four-valve 608cc (37cu in) single as the XT. The SRX was a good-looking bike too, less traditionalist than the SR but with the big single on full display and it was through it that many found their way into single-cylinder racing. A new XT350 was already part of the range by then, with an

all-new dohc four-valve 346cc (21cu in) single. It was a winner, and perhaps underlined the fact that for genuine on/off-road use, a 350 was more manageable than a 600.

By the early 1980s, Yamaha had built successful four-stroke singles and tourers, but had yet to really take the sportsbike market by storm. That came in 1985 with the FZ750. There was much new about the FZ, specifically its liquid-cooled 749cc (46cu in) four, with five valves per cylinder. Over a long development period, Yamaha engineers had experimented with six- and even seven-valve heads before settling on five as the best compromise between power and reliability. The cylinder-block was slanted forward at 45 degrees (the Genesis

concept) to lower the centre of gravity and allow good, straight inlet and exhaust ports, not to mention space for the four down-draught carburettors. It all added up to a very efficient and powerful engine (106bhp, plus a good flat torque curve) that gave Yamaha class leadership for a while. It was followed up in 1987 with the FZR1000 Genesis, whose main innovation was an alloy box section frame known as Deltabox. The latter was a big step forward, giving a lower seat height and far better handling than the steel-framed FZ750. The engine was simply an enlarged 750, though with great attention paid to weight and space saving. Power was 135bhp, with a 266km/h (165mph) top speed.

The addition of EXUP (Exhaust

The 1988 brochure showing part of the XT trail-bike range

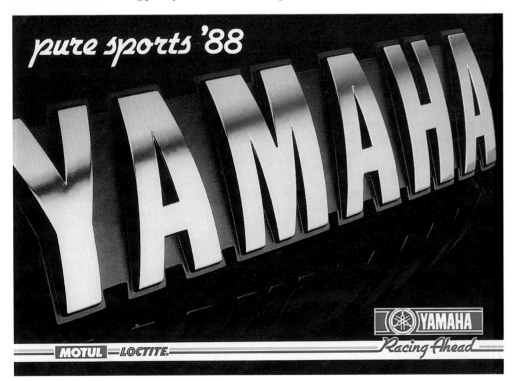

Ultimate Power Valve) in 1989 gave even more power, with a valve in the exhaust collector box to control the gas pressure wave. That same year saw the 750 updated with the alloy frame, plus a new FZR600 to contest the up-and-coming supersports 600 class. It was sobering to realize that the 600 produced 90bhp at 10,500rpm, not much less than the 750 had just four years earlier, and with a mere four valves per cylinder. An FZR400R, to comply with Japanese licencing laws, was another addition to the range. The 600 and 1000 models were updated in 1996 into the fully-faired Thundercat and Thunderace, but here Yamaha seemed to have lost its sporting edge. Where the FZ/FZR were genuinely innovative with strong race influences, the new bikes looked and rode more like softer sports tourers.

New Sport, New Standards

Meanwhile, Yamaha had not forgotten its smaller bikes, and still favoured the two-stroke. The TZR125 of 1988 used a reed-valved two-stroke single together with the latest Deltabox frame. It came with or without a fairing, and was a great success. More intriguing was the TDR250, an attempt at mirroring the big TDM850 with a trail bike style but with road tyres and road performance. The twin-cylinder two-stroke gave an amazing 172km/h (107mph) maximum speed, and the TDR certainly provided an alternative to race replicas. We musn't forget to mention the TDM, which was launched in 1990. It had elements of the sportsbikes, notably the Deltabox, and its 849cc/52cu inch twin-cylinder engine, based around the Genesis five-valve layout, with vaguely trail bike styling. Yamaha called it a 'New Sport' concept, and it is

1998 Drag Star Classic

ABOVE: FZ750

BELOW: The FJ1100 (and 1200) were reliable tourers

The TDM850; not sports, touring or trail, but 'New Sport'

Kenny Roberts on a 1980 TZ750 at Daytona

YAMAHA **FZR600R**

ABOVE: 1984 500cc (31.5cu in) Grand Prix racer

RIGHT: Sales brochure for the FZR600

successful enough to be still on sale at the end of the decade. It also led to the TRX850 offshoot, more of a traditional café racer using the same mechanics. Custom bikes, meanwhile, were becoming more specialized. In the 1970s and early '80s it had been enough to fit high bars and extra chrome to existing twins and fours, but Yamaha's XV535 Virago did much to change this. It managed to look like a big V-twin, but was in fact a simple, cheap-to-run 535cc (32.6cu in) unit, producing a moderate 47bhp, and shaft-drive reduced maintenance as well. Light, low-seated and easy to ride, the Virago was an instant hit. So successful, that it spawned 125, 250, 750 and 1100 versions. And as the 1990s draws to a close, a new market is appearing for luxury scooters. Pioneered by Honda, this has taken off to such an extent that Yamaha and Suzuki have both responded with

versions of their own. Yamaha's Majesty is typical, the 250cc (15cu in) four-stroke allowing main road performance, with added weather protection and lockable luggage built-in.

But for Yamaha, two bikes stand out in the 1990s, and neither are scooters. We've mentioned how the FZR series seemed to lose its way as the Thundercat and Thunderace. The bikes that changed all that were the R1 in 1998, and the R6 of 1999. The R1 is a milestone bike, setting new standards in the one-litre supersports class. It is lighter, smaller and more powerful than any of its rivals, and great play is made of the 'three figures': 150bhp, 177kg and 1,395mm (shortest wheelbase). As Alan Cathcart wrote in *Motorcycle Sport & Leisure*: 'The face of sportbiking has just changed: the new look is red and white (or blue, if you insist) with snake-eye

The FZR Genesis, with Yamaha's 'Genesis' box-section alloy frame on clear display

headlights and works Superbike performance on the road. No compromises.' In fact, the R1 is the first of a new family of supersports bikes, including a 750cc R7 for Superbike racing and a 599cc (36.5cu in) R6. With the R6, Yamaha has done it again. More power (120bhp at 13,000rpm) than any other 600, and it is marginally lighter than them all as well, its top speed being over 274km/h (170mph). For a 'mere' 600, it gives an astonishing performance, and

BELOW: The 1998 R1, which set new standards for one-litre sportsbikes

underlines the fact that Yamaha intends to hold tight to its sportsbike market leadership. One just wonders what organ repairer Torakusu Yamaha would have made of all this.

YANKEE *U.S.A. 1970–74*

An interesting 488cc (30cu in) machine made by coupling two 244cc Ossa two-strokes together, the idea of Ossa's American importer.

YORK *Austria 1927–30*

Jap-powered and made by Omega in England, to a design by Robert Sturm.

YOUNG *England 1919–23*

A 269cc (16cu in) engine for bicycles and a 130cc (8cu in) replacement design sold to Walton Engineering.

YVEL *France 1921–24*

Used own 174/233cc (11/14cu in) engines.

OPPOSITE: Yamaha GTS1000. Note single-sided front suspension

Z

ZANELLA *Argentina 1957–*
Produced mopeds, lightweights and scooters, first built under licence from Ceccato of Italy. Its own designs appeared from 1960, and there were increasing links with Yamaha in the 1990s.

ZEDEL *France 1902–15*
A range of singles and V-twins of 2–3.5hp.

ZEGEMO *Germany 1924–25*
Used bought-in 248cc (15cu in) two-stroke Baumi engines.

ZEHNDER *Switzerland 1923–39*
Various two-strokes up to 248cc (15cu in). The factory was moved to Switzerland by its new owner in the early 1930s.

ZEHNER *Germany 1924–26*
A 197cc (12cu in) sv utility.

ZENIT *Italy 1945–56*
Used 123/174cc (7.5/11cu in) AMC engines.

ZENITH *England 1907–49*
First used a 482cc (29cu in) sv single, but the big breakthrough came with Gradua gear from 1908, giving a variable-gear ratio when most machines had fixed single-speed. This gave it a huge advantage in competition from which the Zenith Gradua was notoriously banned. Used mostly V-twin JAPs from 1914, and 1922 saw more conventional chain-drive bikes with JAP, Bradshaw and Blackburne engines. Production ceased in 1931 when Zenith changed hands, followed by limited production which finally ceased for good in 1949.

ABOVE and OPPOSITE: 1914 Zenith 550cc (34cu in) V-twin. The engine is a JAP

ZEPHYR *England 1922–23*
A 131cc (8cu in) two-stroke clip-on.

ZETA *Italy 1948–54*
A small-wheeled scooter type, with bought-in 48/60cc (3/4cu in) engines.

ZETGE *Germany 1922–25*
Used both DKW two-strokes to 173cc (11cu in) and its own of similar capacity.

ZEUGNER *Germany 1903–06*
Used a wide variety of bought-in engines, including units from FN and Peugeot.

ZEUS *Czechoslovakia 1902–12*
Produced singles (3–3.5hp) and V-twins (4–4.5hp) and also sold under the Linser brand name.

ZEUS *Germany 1925–27*
Used Küchen three-valve ohc singles to 498cc (30cu in).

ZIEJANÜ *Germany 1924–26*
211/246cc (13/15cu in) two-strokes and 348/498cc (21/30cu in) sv and ohv JAP four-strokes.

ZIRO *Germany 1919–24*
Disc-valved two-strokes of 148 and 346cc (9 and 21cu in).

ZÜNDAPP *Germany 1921–84*
The company began relatively late with a copy of the 211cc (13cu in) two-stroke Levis, but at one time came to be the leading German manufacturer. By 1930 it was building its own range of two-strokes of up to 300cc (18cu in) and had built 100,000 machines by 1933. The first four-

1939 Zündapp KS750 746cc (45.5cu in) flat twin with Stoppa Sidecar

A beautifully restored 1958 600cc (37cu in) Zündapp, with swinging arm frame and high-rise bars

stroke used the Rudge Python four-valve single but it introduced its own four-strokes in 1933, flat twins of 398/498cc (24/30cu in) and 598/797cc (36/49cu in) flat fours. Designed by Richard and Xavier Küchen, all had pressed steel frames and shaft-drive. There were new 198/348cc (12/21cu in) unit-construction two-strokes, also with pressed steel frames and shaft-driven and the KS750 flat twin was built during the war (during which time the 250,000th Zündapp was made). After the war it resumed with the 198cc two-stroke and 597cc flat twin. New post-war products were a 48cc (3cu in) clip-on and the 147cc (9cu in) Bella scooter in 1953, as well as lightweight two-strokes expanded up to 247cc (15cu in). A wide range of air- and water-cooled two-strokes (road and off-road) continued into the 1980s, but Zündapp was unable to survive, and closed in 1984.

Zündapp KS175 on display: smart but not enough to keep the company going

ZÜRTZ-REKORD *Germany 1922–26*
A variety of power units were used, from the 142cc (9cu in) DKW to 490cc (30cu in) JAP, all using a wide top-tube frame which acted as a fuel tank.

ZWEIRAD-UNION *Germany 1958–74*
Faced with a declining market, a number of German manufacturers (DKW, Express, Victoria and later Hercules) merged to form Zweirad-Union. Despite rationalization, the combine itself eventually succumbed to takeover by Fichtel & Sachs in 1969.

ZWERG *Germany 1924–25*
Used own 147/187cc (9/11cu in) two-strokes.

ZWI *Israel 1952–55*
Produced 123cc (7.5cu in) Villiers or JAP-engined machines.

ZZR *Poland 1960–*
Produces mopeds only, under the Komar brand name.

BELOW and RIGHT: Zündapp's shaft-driven flat twins were remarkably similar to contemporary BMWs, the only difference being that, from the 1950s, Zündapp tried selling smaller, cheaper machines

Bibliography

An encyclopedia can never be more than a collection of summaries. For fuller details of the better-known marques, it is worth tracking down the books listed below, all of which were referred to when preparing this work.

Aermacchi, by Mick Walker
  (Transport Source Books)
Benelli, by Mick Walker
  (Transport Source Books)
BSA Singles Gold Portfolio
  (Brooklands Books)
BSA Competition History,
  by Norman Vanhouse (Haynes Publishing)
BSA: The Complete Story,
  by Owen Wright (Crowood Press)
Ducati Supersport,
  by Ian Falloon (Haynes Publishing)
The Ducati Story,
  by Ian Falloon (Haynes Publishing)
Gilera Road Racers,
  by Raymond Ainscoe (Osprey)
Harley-Davidson Classics 1903–65,
  by Jerry Hatfield (Motorbooks International)
Inside Harley-Davidson,
  by Jerry Hatfield (Motorbooks International)
The Harley-Davidson Motor Company,
  by David Wright (Motorbooks International)
Honda: The Early Classic Motorcycles,
  by Roy Bacon (Niton Publishing)
The Humber Story,
  by A.B. Demaus & T.C. Tarring (Sutton Publishing)
The Indian,
  by Tod Rafferty
(Bramley Books)

Kawasaki,
  by Mick Walker (Osprey)
Kawasaki Fours,
  by Mick Walker (Crowood Press)
Lambretta: An Illustrated History,
  by Nigel Cox (Haynes Publishing)
Laverda Gold Portfolio
  (Brooklands Books)
Moto Guzzi,
  by Mick Walker (Osprey)
Moto Guzzi V-twins,
  by Mick Walker (Crowood Press)
MZ,
  by Mick Walker (Transport Source Books)
Norton Rotaries,
  by Kris Perkins (Osprey)
Norton,
  by Mick Woollett
Royal Enfield,
  by Anne Bradford (Amulree Publications)
Suzuki,
  by Roy Bacon (Chartwell Books)
Suzuki, by Mick Walker
  (Osprey)
Triumph Triples,
  by Andrew Morland & Peter Henshaw (Osprey)
Vespa: An Illustrated History,
  by Eric Brockway (Haynes Publishing)
The Victory Motorcycle,
  by Michael Dapper & Lee Klancher (Motobooks International)
Vincent,
  by Duncan Wherret (Osprey)
Yamaha, by Mick Walker
  (Osprey)

British Motorcycles of the 1940s & 1950s,
  by Roy Bacon (Osprey)
British Motorcycles of the 1960s,
  by Roy Bacon (Osprey)
The Encyclopedia of Motorcycles,
  by Roland Brown (Lorenz Books)
Whatever Happened to the British Motorcycle Industry?
  by Bert Hopwood (Haynes Publishing)
Well Made in America,
  by Peter Reid (McGraw Hill)
Motorcycle Milestones Vol 1,
  by Richard Renstrom (Classics Unlimited)
Motor Scooters Colour Family Album,
  by Andrea & David Sparrow (Veloce Publishing)
The Illustrated Encyclopedia of Motorcycles,
  by Erwin Tragatsch (Hamlyn)
Superbike Specials of the 1970s,
  by Mick Walker (Windrow & Greene)
The History of Motorcycles,
  by Mick Walker (Hamlyn)
Great British Bikes,
  by Ian Ward & Laurie Caddell (Tiger Books International)
The Encyclopedia of the Motorcycle,
  by Hugo Wilson (Dorling Kindersley)
British Motorcycles since 1950 (Vols 1–6),
  by Steve Wilson (Haynes Publishing)

A 1948 customized Harley-Davidson 747cc (46cu in) WLC